Songbook 9.0 Table of Contents

A Greater Song

Written by
PAUL BALOCHE and MATT REDMAN

6

Hal - le - lu - jah, we want to lift You higher, Hal - le - lu - jah,
we want to lift You higher, Hal - le - lu - jah, we want to lift You higher,
Hal - le - lu - jah, we want to lift You higher, Hal - le - lu - jah,
1. we want to lift You higher.
2. we want to lift You higher.

Chords Used in This Song

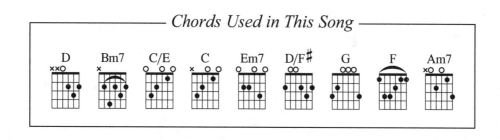

D   Bm7   C/E   C   Em7   D/F#   G   F   Am7

All We Need

Words and Music by
CHARLIE HALL

8

and all___ we need is You,___ All___

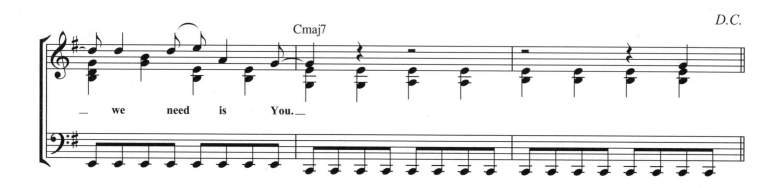

D.C.

___ we need is You.___

⊕ CODA

we have all___ we need in You,___ and all___

1.

___ we need is You,___ all___ we need is You.___ 'Cause

2.

we need is You.___ all_____ we need is You.

all___ we need___   is___ You.___

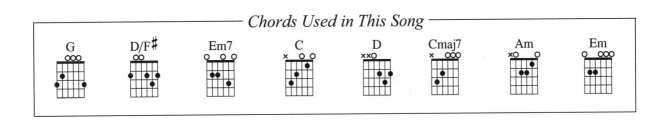

Adoration
(Down In Adoration Falling)

Capo 1 (C)

Words and music by THOMAS AQUINAS
Additional Verse and Chorus by MATT MAHER

Down in ad-o-ra-tion fall-ing, this great sac-ra-ment we hail; o-ver an-cient forms de-part-ing, new-er rites of grace pre-vail; faith for all de-fects sup-ply-ing where the fee-ble sens-es fail.

16

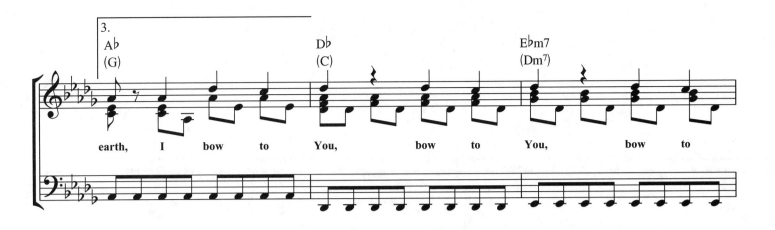

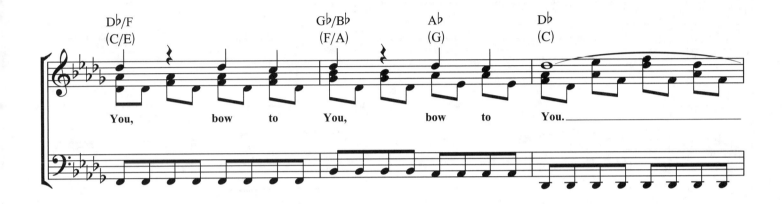

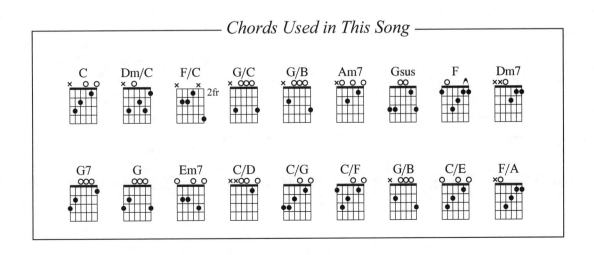

Chords Used in This Song

All Over the World

Words and Music by
MATT REDMAN and
MARTIN SMITH

20

all o - ver the world._____

All o - ver the world___

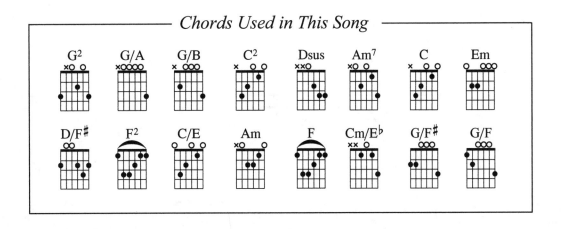

Chords Used in This Song

Almighty God

Capo 1 (A)

Words and Music by
TIM HUGHES

Moderate Rock ♩ = 88

1. The ris - ing Sun that fills the sky, the star - ry___ host
2. The vast ex - panse of earth and sea, held by___ You

that lights the night,_____ re - flect - ing Your glo - ry.
in har - mo - ny,_____ speaks of Your glo - ry.

The moun - tain heights, for - ev - er stand, the rain that__ falls
All You've made, since time be - gan, life it - self;

to soak the land,_____ re - spond to Your glo -
Your per - fect plan,_____ and it's all for Your glo -

As We Seek Your Face

Words and Music by
DAVE BILBROUGH

Awesome Is The Lord Most High

Words and Music by
CHRIS TOMLIN, JESSE REEVES,
CARY PIERCE and JON ABEL

Great are You,___ Lord,   might - y___ in strength.___
Where You send___ us,   God we___ will go.

___   You are faith - ful,   and
___   You're the an - swer,   we

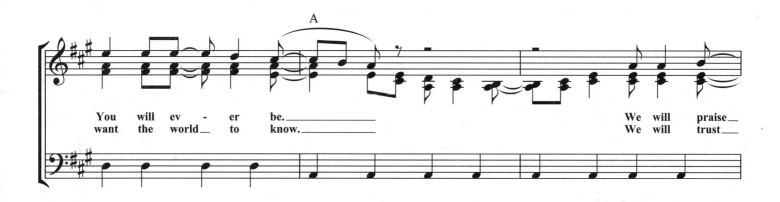

You will ev - er be.___   We will praise___
want the world___ to know.___   We will trust___

___ You   all of___ our days,___
___ You   when You call___ our name,

now and for-ev - er. How awe - some_ is the

To CODA ⊕

Lord most high.____

Hal - le-lu - jah, hal - le-lu - jah, how

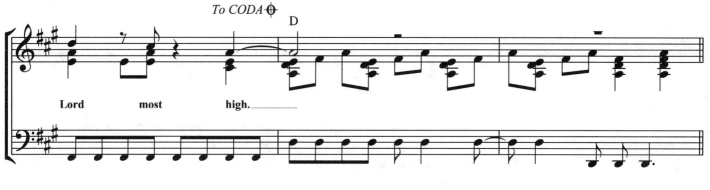

awe - some_ is the Lord most high.____

Hal - le-lu - jah,

We will praise You to-geth - er, for now and_ for - ev - er.____ How awe - some_ is the Lord most high,____ the Lord most high.

Chords Used in This Song

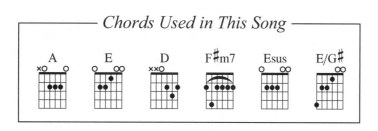

A   E   D   F#m7   Esus   E/G#

Be Lifted High

Words and Music by
LEELAND MOORING

Beautiful Lord

Words and Music by
LEELAND MOORING and MARC BYRD

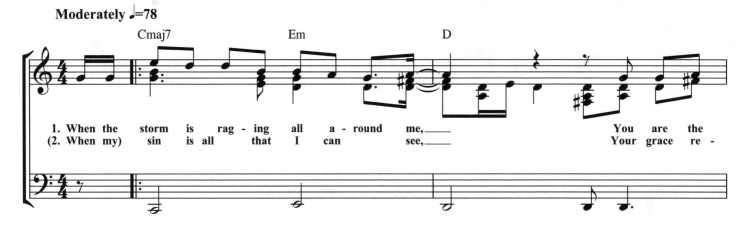

1. When the storm is rag - ing all a - round me, You are the
(2. When my) sin is all that I can see, Your grace re -

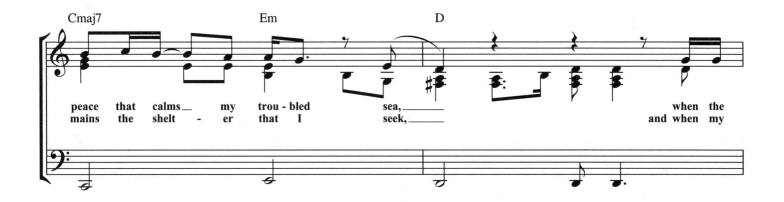

peace that calms my trou - bled sea, when the
mains the shelt - er that I seek, and when my

cares of this world dark - en my day, You are the
weak - ness is all I can give, Your gen - tle

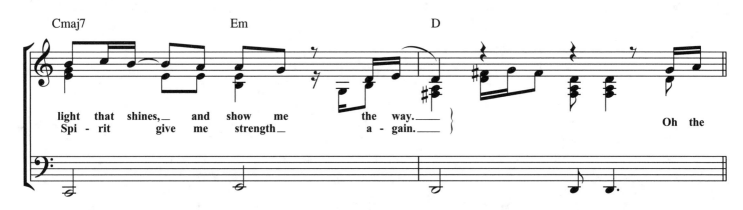

light that shines, and show me the way.
Spi - rit give me strength a - gain.
Oh the

mer - cy that has made me free.____ Oh the

CODA

You're beau - ti - ful,____ my Lord.__

You're beau - ti - ful,____ my Lord.__

You're beau - ti - ful.____

Chords Used in This Song

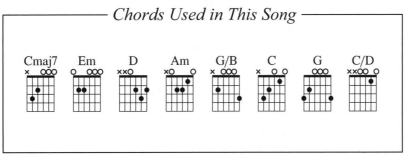

Carried To The Table

Words and Music by
LEELAND MOORING,
MARC BYRD and STEVE HINDALONG

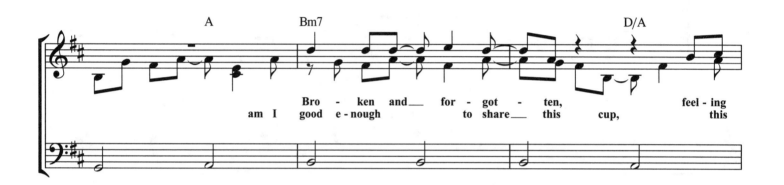

46

Closer

Words and Music by CHARLIE HALL,
KENDALL COMBES, DUSTIN RAGLAND
and BRIAN BERGMAN

Center

Words and Music by
**CHARLIE HALL
and MATT REDMAN**

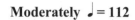

Oh,___ Christ,___ be the cen - ter of___ our lives,

___ be the place___ we fix___ our eyes,___ be the cen-

- ter of___ our lives.___ And You're the

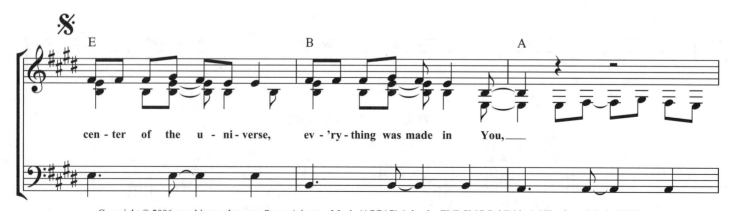

cen - ter of the u - ni - verse, ev - 'ry - thing was made in You,___

53

54

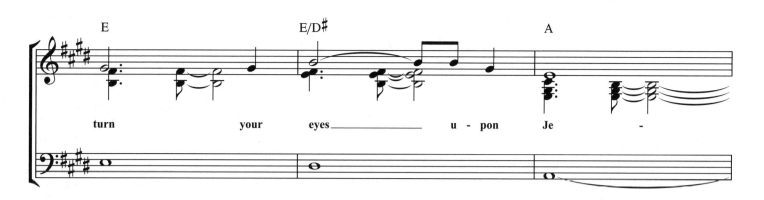

turn your eyes_____ u - pon Je -

(a cappella)   *(B)*

sus,_____ and look full in His won - der - ful face.

𝅗𝅥 = 𝅘𝅥𝅭, **Slowing to end**

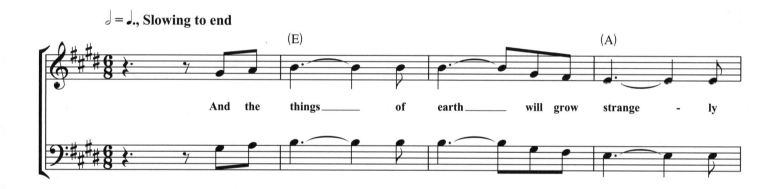

And the things_____ of earth_____ will grow strange - ly

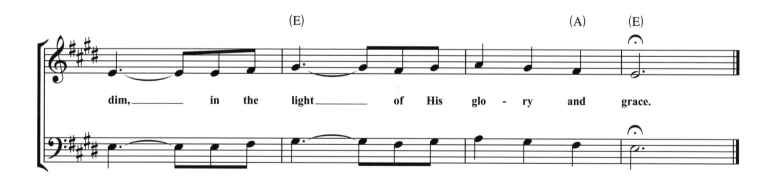

dim,_____ in the light_____ of His glo - ry and grace.

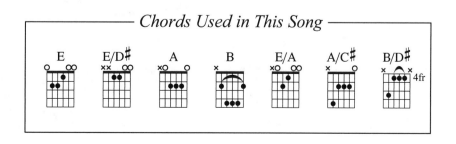

Chords Used in This Song

E E/D♯ A B E/A A/C♯ B/D♯

*Chord symbols to end reflect implied harmony.

Communion

Words and Music by
MAC POWELL, DAVID CARR,
TAI ANDERSON, BRAD AVERY
and MARK LEE

60

This is the bod-

This is the bod - y,_____

this is the blood._____

This is the bod -

- y,_____

this is the blood._____

Chords Used in This Song

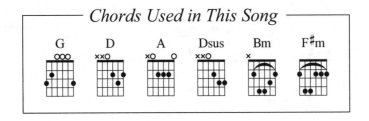

G   D   A   Dsus   Bm   F#m

Declare Victory
(Canticle Of Zechariah)

Words and Music by
MATT MAHER and TAM LE

Capo 1 (G)

Keyboard
(Guitar)

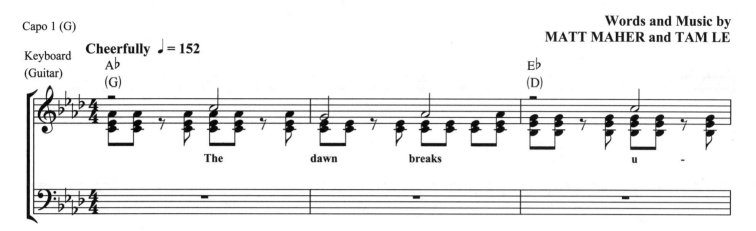

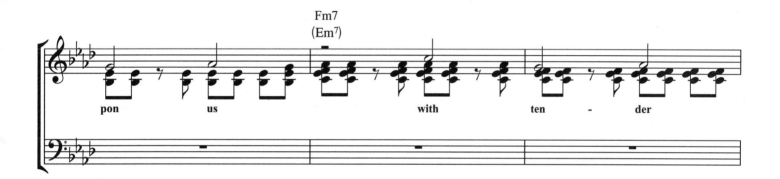

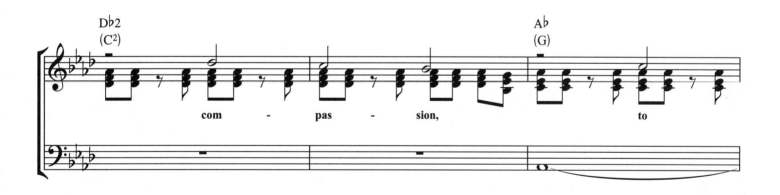

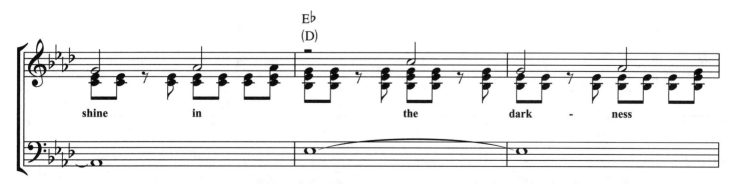

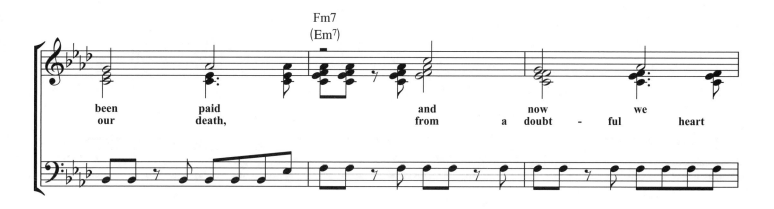

been   paid   and   now   we
our   death,   from   a   doubt - ful   we   heart

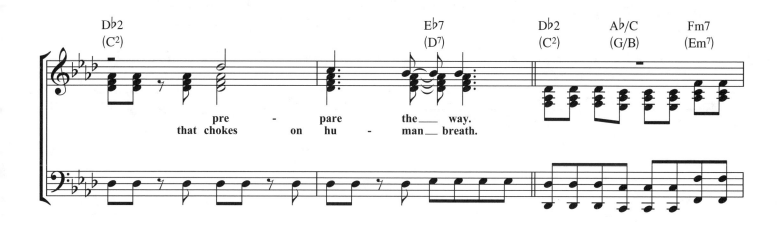

pre -   pare   the___ way.
that chokes   on hu -   man___ breath.

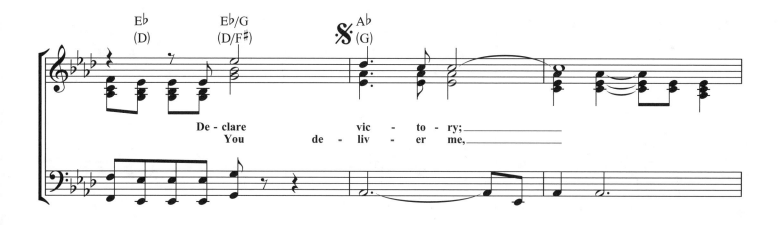

De - clare   vic - to - ry;_____
You   de - liv - er me,_____

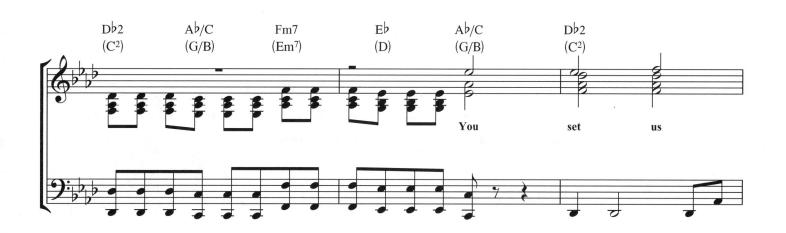

You   set   us

66

68

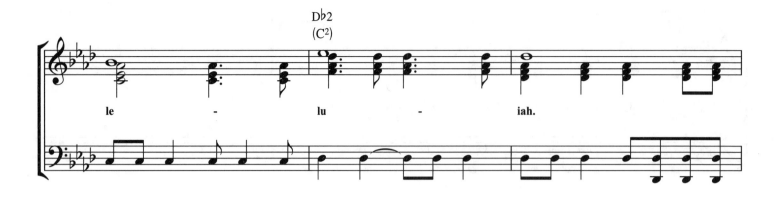

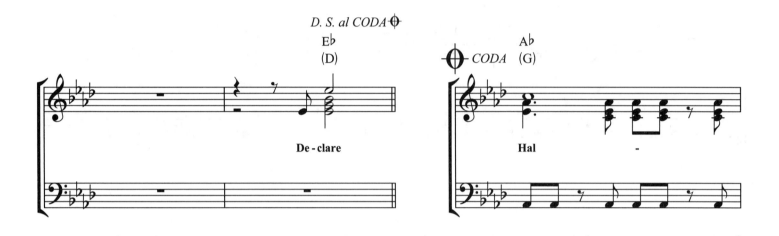

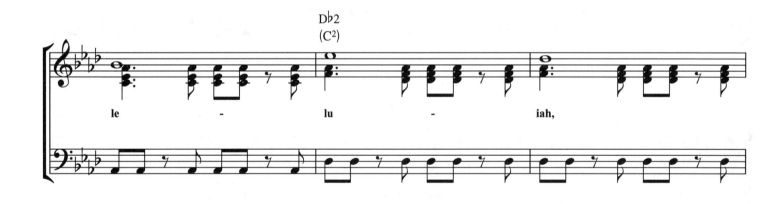

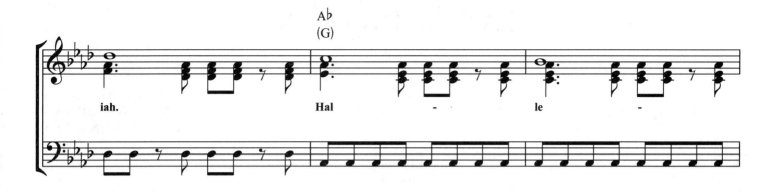

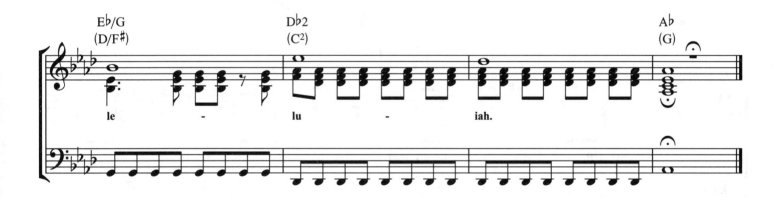

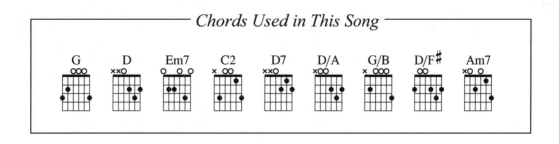

Chords Used in This Song

Everlasting God

Words and Music by
BRENTON BROWN
and KEN RILEY

*All chords in brackets are optional.

71

74

You do not faint, You won't grow wea-ry. You're the de-fend-er of the weak, You com-fort those in need. You lift us up on wings like ea-gles.

Chords Used in This Song

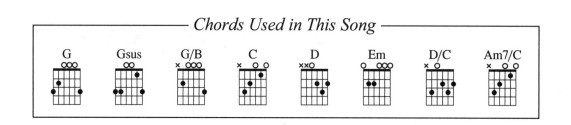

G   Gsus   G/B   C   D   Em   D/C   Am7/C

Everything Glorious

**Words and Music by
DAVID CROWDER**

76

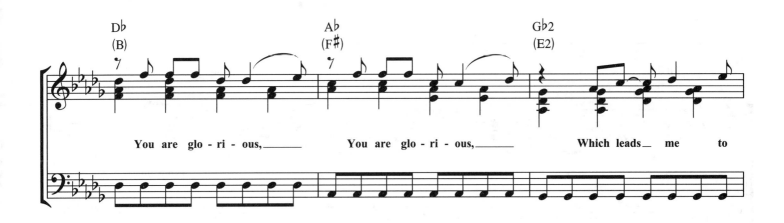

78

Chords Used in This Song

Everything

Words and Music by
TIM HUGHES

CODA

Chords Used in This Song

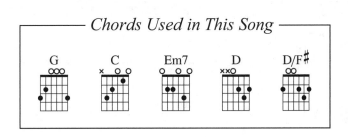

Give Me Jesus

**Words and Music by
JEREMY CAMP**

86

Give You Glory

Words and Music by
JEREMY CAMP

Moderately fast, ♩ = 132

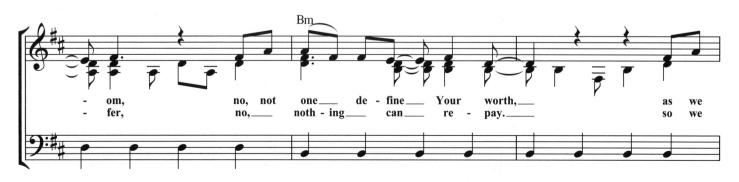

G   Gm

wor - thy, ___ we just want ___ to touch ___ Your heart ___ Lord, touch ___

D

___ Your heart. ___ Glo - ry, ___ lift - ing up our voice and sing - ing

Bm   G

Ho - ly, ___ You a - lone ___ are wor - thy, ___

Gm

we just want ___ to touch ___ Your heart ___ Lord, touch ___ Your heart. ___

D   Bm

Glo - ry, ___ sing - ing Ho - ly, ___ We're sing - ing

2nd time, voc. ad. lib.

92

wor - thy,___ we want___ to touch___ Your heart,___ Lord, touch___

___ Your heart.___ ___ Your heart.___ Glo - ry,___

___ oh.___

Glo - ry.___

Chords Used in This Song

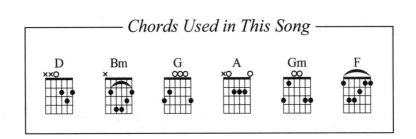

Great God Of Wonders

**Words and Music by
ANDY BROMLEY**

94

praise,_____

praise,_____

praise._____

1., D.S.

To CODA ⊕

D.C.
(Take repeat)

2.

You are the great God a-

bove all___ gods, You are the great King a-

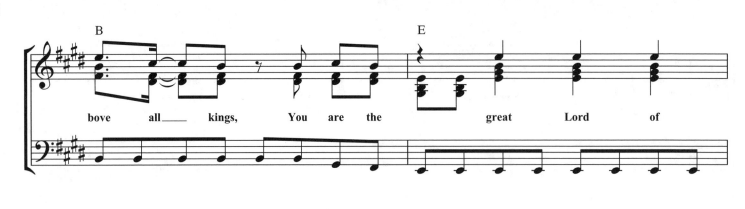

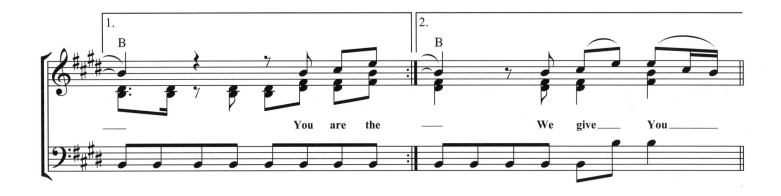

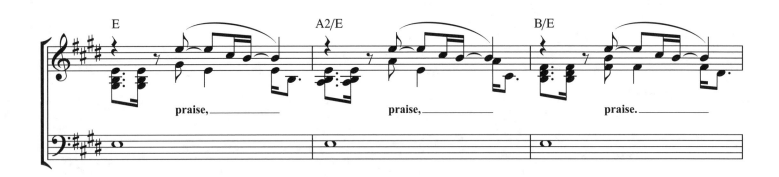

D.S. al CODA
(take 1st ending)

praise._____ We give You_____

CODA

Free, slowly

On - ly____ Lord, wor - thy all our praise Lord Je - sus.

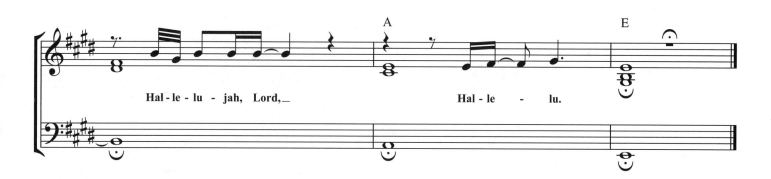

Hal - le - lu - jah, Lord,__ Hal - le - lu.

Chords Used in This Song

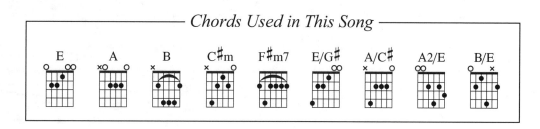

E   A   B   C#m   F#m7   E/G#   A/C#   A2/E   B/E

God Of Justice

Words and Music by
TIM HUGHES

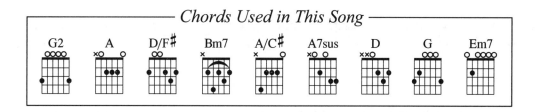

Hallelujah God Is Near

Words and Music by
ROBBIE SEAY, RYAN OWENS
DAN HAMILTON
and TAYLOR JOHNSON

104

106

Hosanna (Praise Is Rising)

Words and Music by
BRENTON BROWN and PAUL BALOCHE

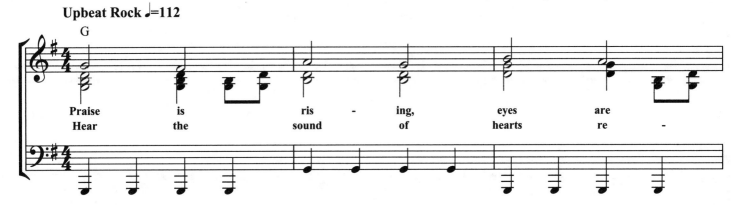

Praise is rising, eyes are
Hear the sound of hearts re-

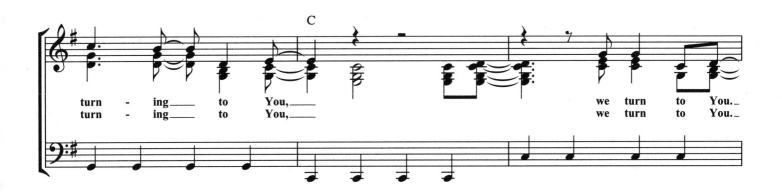

turn-ing to You, we turn to You.
turn-ing to You, we turn to You.

Hope is
In Your

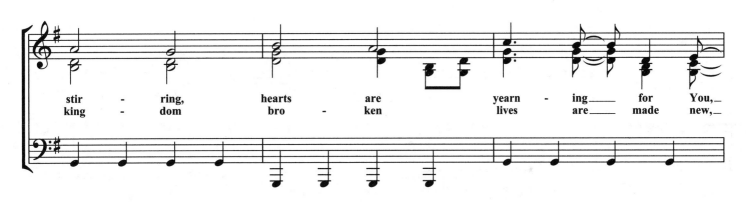

stir-ring, hearts are yearn-ing for You,
king-dom bro-ken lives are made new,

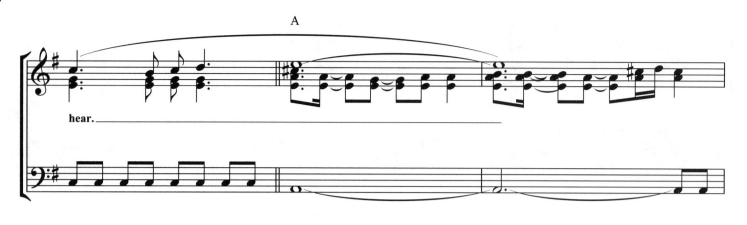

hear.

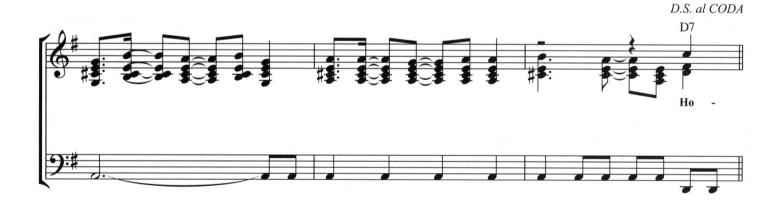

D.S. al CODA

D7

Ho -

CODA

C   G/C

Yeah,   You are the God who saves

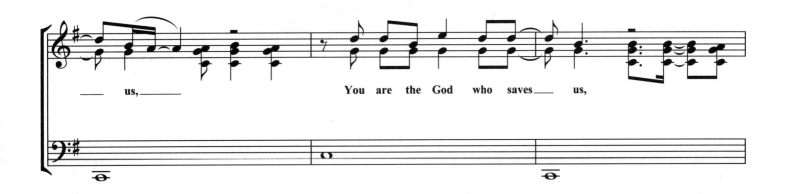

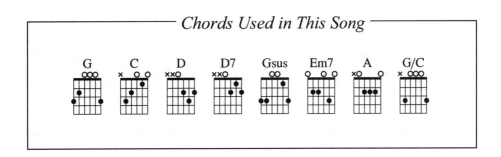

Chords Used in This Song

Hear Our Song

**Words and Music by
JADON LAVIK, STEVE HINDALONG
and MARC BYRD**

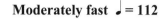

In (1., 3.) joy - ous___ sur - ren - der, with___ our
(2.) joy - ous___ sur - ren - der, with___ our

eyes fixed on You,___ may our lives bring You glo - ry,
hearts full of praise, we sing of Your mer - cy,

to serve You_ in all that we do.
we sing of___ Your love and Your grace.
2. In

And (1., 2.) Fa - ther,___ hear our___ song,___
(3.) Fa - ther,___ we have_ come,___

to of-fer__ our lives __ to the Ho-ly__ One.__
-fer,_____ You are ho - ly.)_____

__ And we live_____ for Your glo-

-ry, and we live_____ by Your love,__ and we sing_

__ of Your glo - ry, and we sing__ of Your love.__

Chords Used in This Song

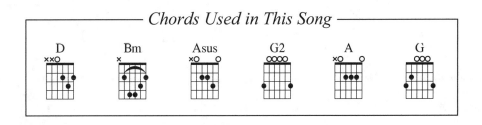

How Can I Keep From Singing

Words and Music by
CHRIS TOMLIN, MATT REDMAN
and ED CASH

118

sing. Yeah,_____ I can__

_____ sing._____

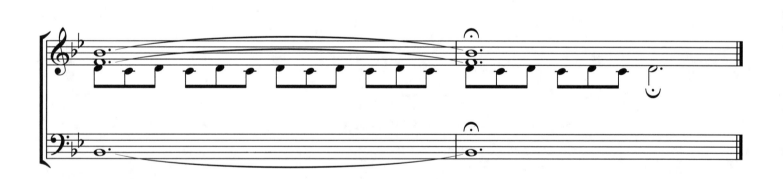

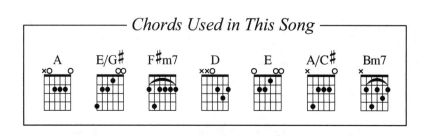

Chords Used in This Song

A   E/G#   F#m7   D   E   A/C#   Bm7

I Will Remember You

Words and Music by
BRENTON BROWN

Chords Used in This Song

Jesus You Are Worthy

Words and Music by
BRENTON BROWN

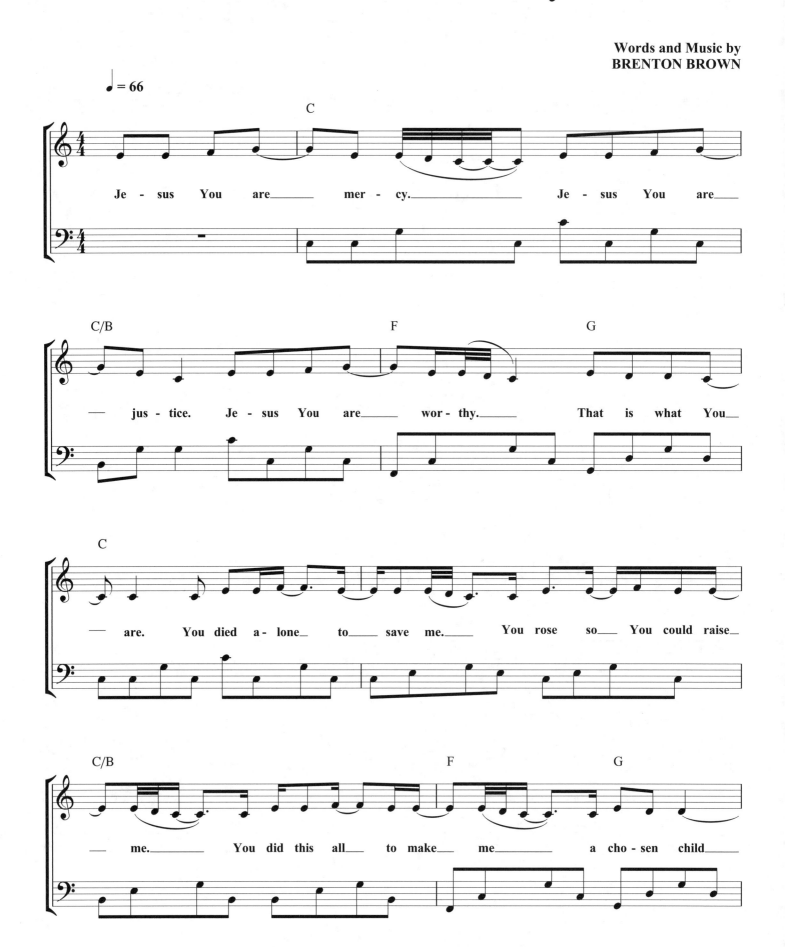

deeds,   You suf-fered si - lent-ly   the on - ly guilt-less

man   in all of his-to-ry.____   How wor-thy is the

D.S. al CODA 𝄋

⊕ CODA

____ wor- thy.____   That is what You____ are.____   Je - sus You are____

____ wor- thy.____   That is what You____ are.

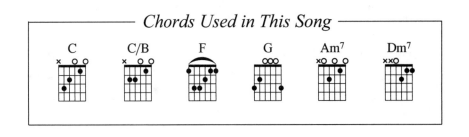

Chords Used in This Song

C   C/B   F   G   Am⁷   Dm⁷

Let God Arise

Words and Music by
CHRIS TOMLIN, ED CASH
and JESSE REEVES

134

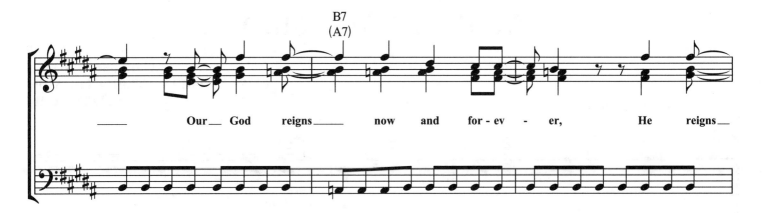

Our God reigns___ now and for-ev-er, He reigns___

___ now and for-ev-er. God a-rise___ er.___

Play 4 times

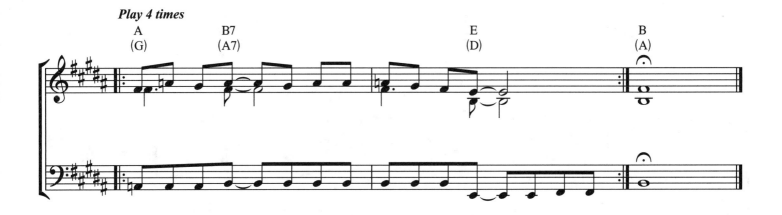

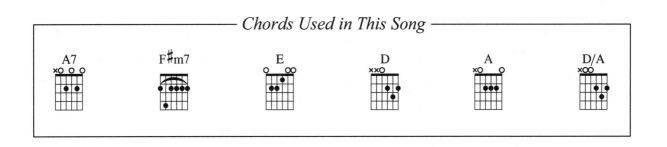

Chords Used in This Song

Made To Worship

**Words and Music by
CHRIS TOMLIN, STEPHAN SHARP
and ED CASH**

Chords Used in This Song

Outrageous Grace
(There's a lot of Pain)

Words and Music by
GODFREY BIRTILL

Ready For You

Words and Music by
JON MICAH SUMRALL

Chords Used in This Song

Resurrection Day

**Words and Music by
MATT MAHER**

1. It's the weight of Your glo-ry, brings the proud to their knees, and the light of rev-e-la-tion, lets the blind man see. It's the pow-er of the cross, breaks a-way death's em-brace,
2. You de-clare what is ho-ly, You de-clare what is good, in the sight of all the na-tions, You de-clare that You are God. It's the pow-er in Your Blood, breaks a-way sin's em-brace,

res - ur - rec - tion___ day.

Resurrection Hymn
(See What a Morning)

Words and Music by
STUART TOWNEND and
KEITH GETTY

Victoriously ♩. = 94

1. See,_____ what the morn - ing, glo - rious-ly bright, with the
2. See_____ Mar - y weep - ing, "Where_____ is He laid?" As in
3. One_____ with the Fa - ther, An - cient of Days, through the

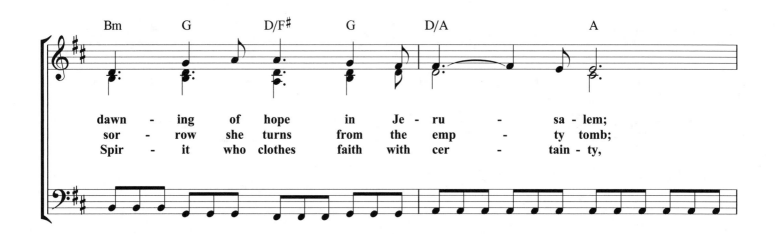

dawn - ing of hope in Je - ru - sa - lem;
sor - row she turns from the emp - ty tomb;
Spir - it who clothes faith with cer - tain - ty,

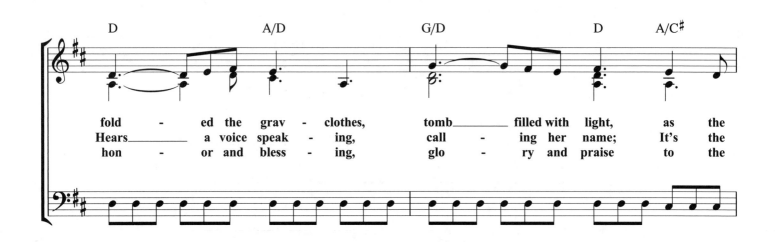

fold - ed the grav - clothes, tomb_____ filled with light, as the
Hears_____ a voice speak - ing, call - ing her name; It's the
hon - or and bless - ing, glo - ry and praise to the

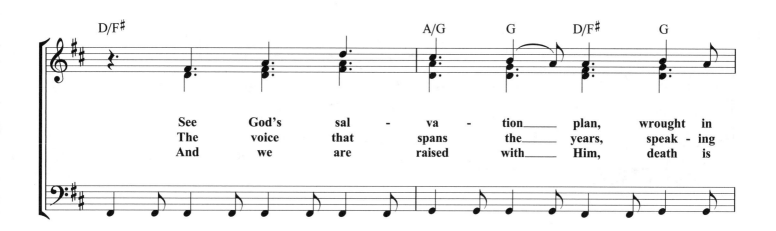

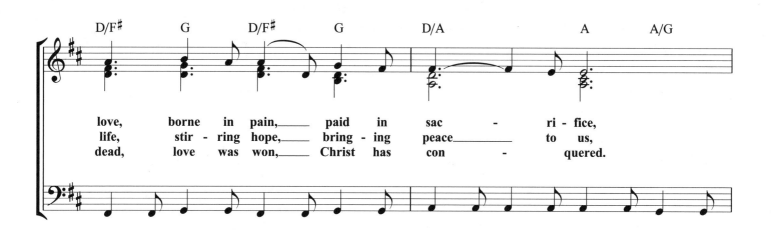

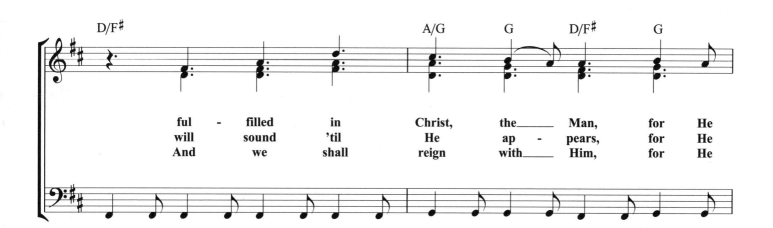

154

lives: Christ   is   ris - en   from the   dead!_____
lives,   Christ   is   ris - en   from the   dead!_____
lives,   Christ   is   ris - en   from the   dead!_____

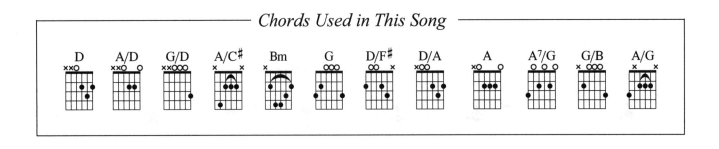

Chords Used in This Song

Unwavering

Words and Music by
MATT MAHER

158

feet, _____ send us out to be

Your hands and__

_____ feet.

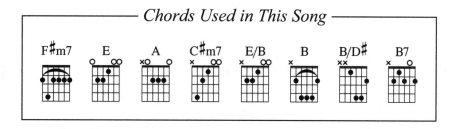

Chords Used in This Song

F#m7   E   A   C#m7   E/B   B   B/D#   B7

See His Love

Words and Music by
TOM LOCKLEY

Double Rock Feel ♩ = 72

1. See His love nail - ed to a cross,___ per - fect and
2. Great - er love no one could ev - er show.___ Mer - cy so

blame - less life_____ giv - en as sac - ri - fice.___ See Him there all in the
un - de - served,___ free - dom I should not know.___ All my sin, all of my

name of Love,___ bro - ken, yet glo - ri - ous,_____ all for the
hid - den shame_____ died with Him on the cross.___ E - ter - ni - ty

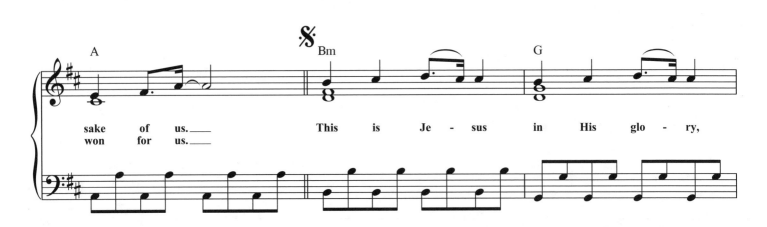

sake of us.___ This is Je - sus in His glo - ry,
won for us.___

Shine

Words and Music by
MATT REDMAN

164

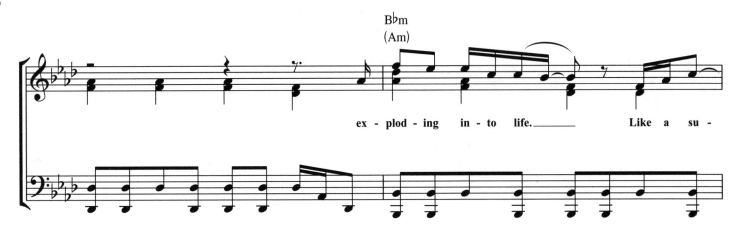

ex - plod - ing in - to life._____ Like a su -

- per - no - va's light,___ Set your Ho - ly Church on fire,_____

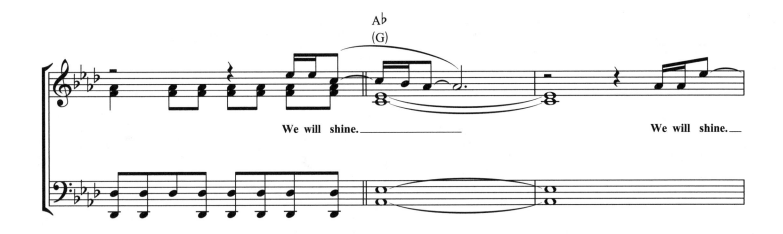

We will shine._____ We will shine.___

D.S. al CODA
(take 2nd repeat)

We will shine___

Son Of God

**Words and Music by
TIM NEUFELD, JON NEUFELD,
ED CASH and GORDON COCHRAN**

170

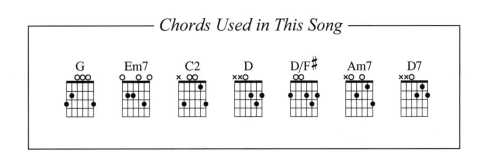

Chords Used in This Song

Sound Of Melodies

Words and Music by
LEELAND MOORING, JACK MOORING
and STEVE WILSON

Moderately, ♩. = 82

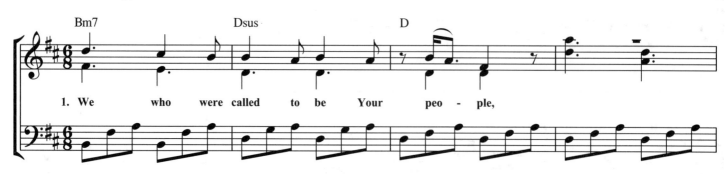

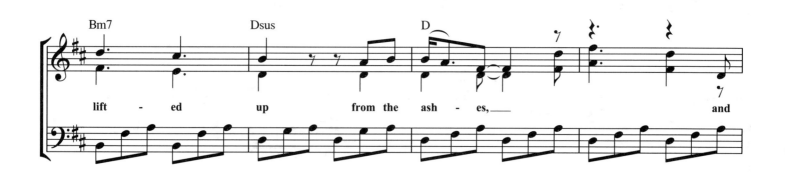

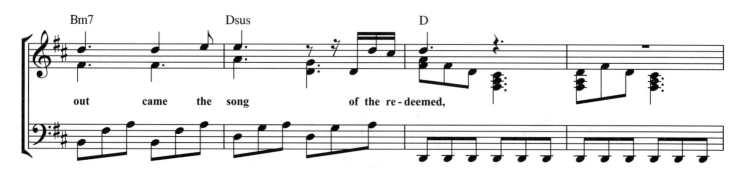

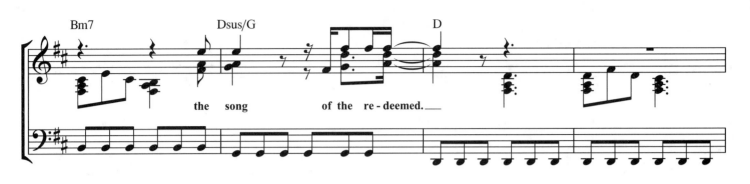

the song of the re-deemed.____

Can you hear the sound of mel-o-dies, oh, the

sound of mel-o-dies ris-ing up to You, ris-ing

up to You, God? The sound of mel-o-dies, oh, the

sound of mel-o-dies ris-ing up to You, ris-ing

174

176

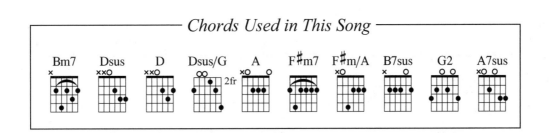

Speak, O Lord

Words and Music by
KEITH GETTY and STUART TOWNEND

Repeat 2 times

deeds of____ faith. Speak, O Lord, and ful - fill_____ in us___ all your
thor - i - ty. Words of power that can ne - ver fail;___ Let their
walk with___ us. Speak, O Lord, till Your church___ is built___ and the

pur - pos - es,___ for Your glo - ry.
truth_____ pre - vail___ o - ver un - be - lief.
earth_____ is filled___ with your glo - ry.

Chords Used in This Song

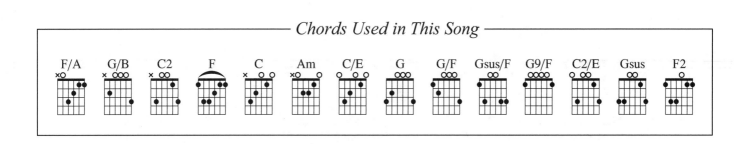

Strong Tower

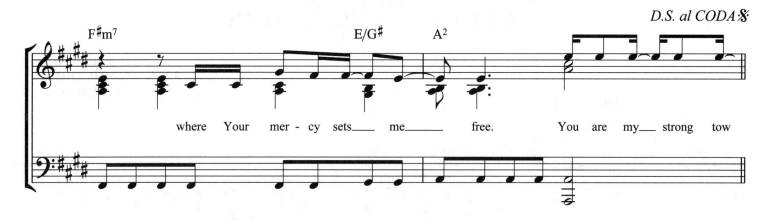

D.S. al CODA 𝄋

where Your mer - cy sets___ me___ free. You are my___ strong tow

CODA

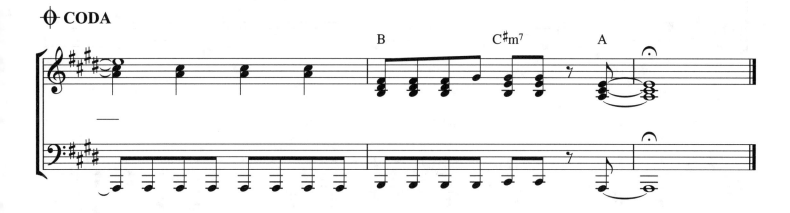

Chords Used in This Song

Tears Of The Saints

Words and Music by
LEELAND MOORING
and JACK MOORING

Moderately ♩ = 92

Capo 4 (G)

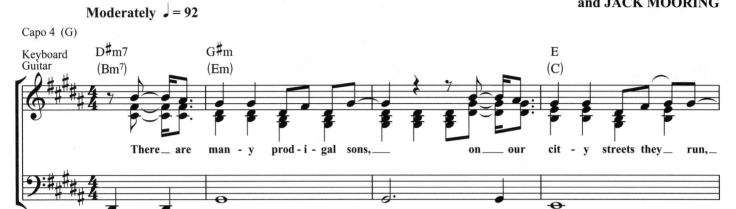

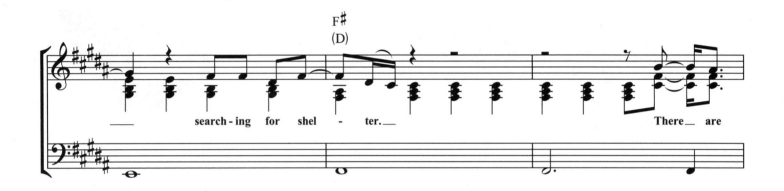

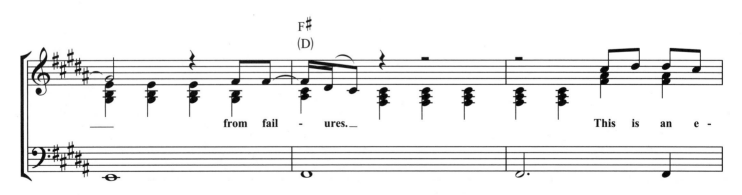

188

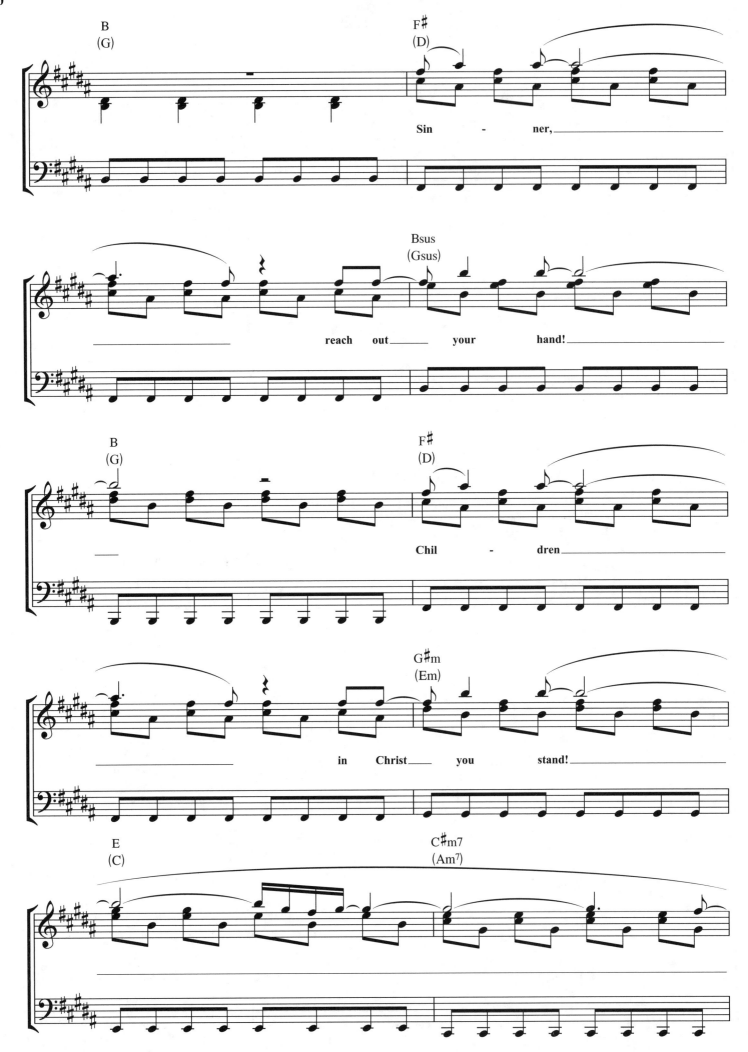

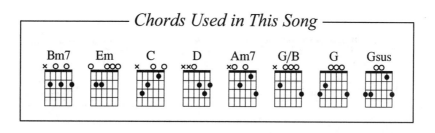

Unashamed

Words and Music by
TIM NEUFELD
and DOUG MCKELVEY

Moderate Rock ♩ = 160

Capo 1 (E)

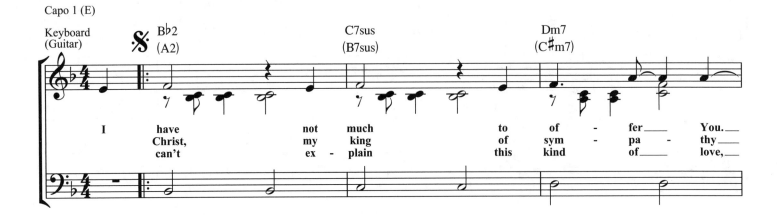

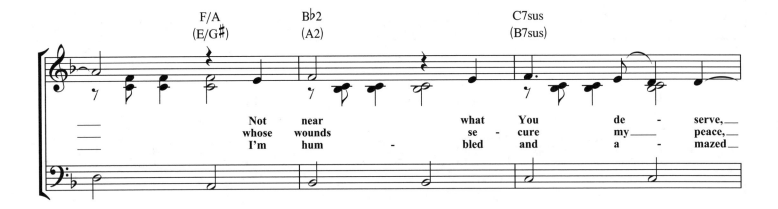

3rd time to Coda ⊕

196

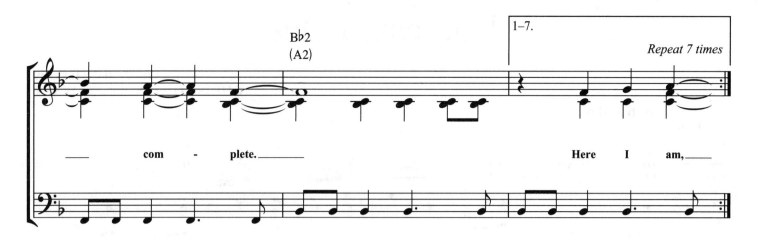

Bb2
(A2)

1–7.

Repeat 7 times

___ com - plete._____ Here I am,_____

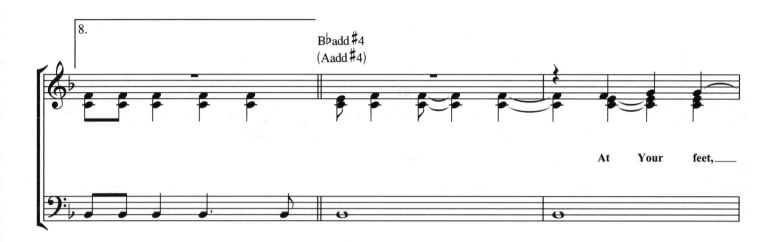

8.

Bbadd#4
(Aadd#4)

At Your feet,_____

rall.

___ I'm com - plete._____

Chords Used in This Song

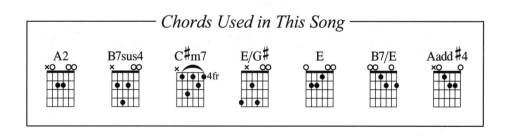

A2   B7sus4   C#m7   E/G#   E   B7/E   Aadd#4

Uncreated One

Words and Music by
CHRIS TOMLIN and J.D. WALT

202

203

While You Were Sleeping

Words and Music by
MARK HALL

208

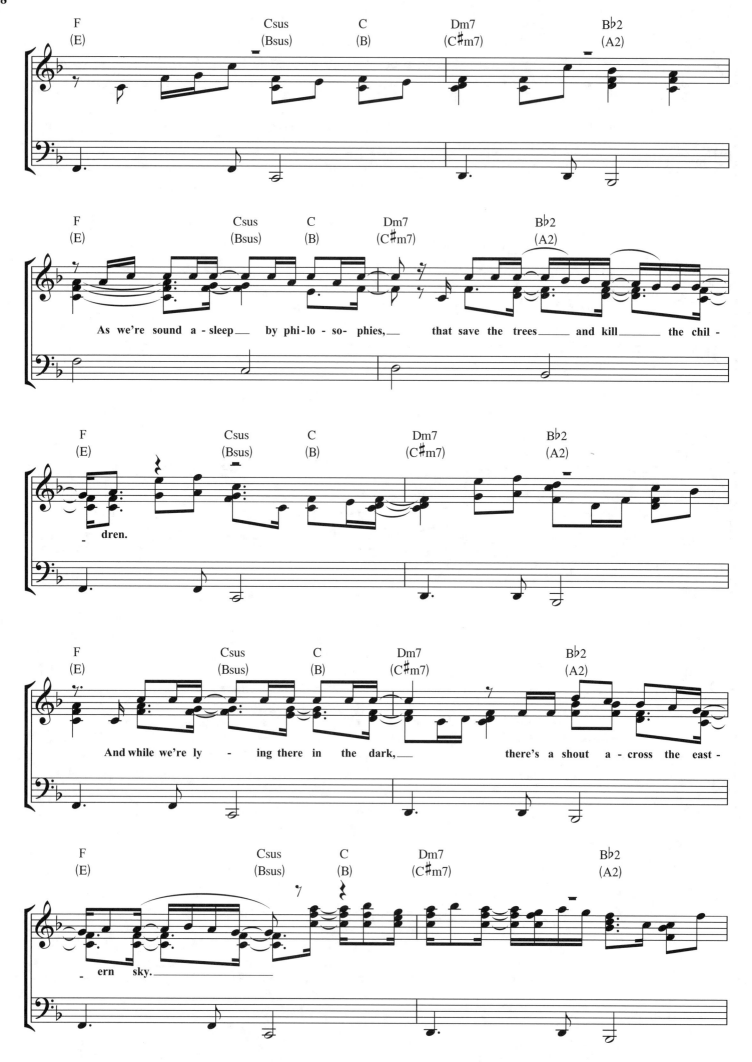

D.S. al CODA 2

CODA 2

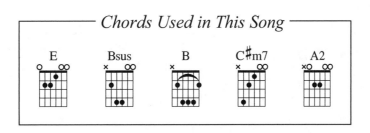

Chords Used in This Song

Wholly Yours

Words and Music by
DAVID CROWDER

214

216

Yes You Have

Words and Music by
**LEELAND MOORING, JACK MOORING
and MATT BRONLEEWE**

218

220

221

yes, You have!___ You've sto - len my heart,___

yes, You have!___ You've wiped a - way___ the stains,___

and broke a - way___ the chains,___ yes, You have!___

1.
You've sto - len my heart,___ ___

2.

Chords Used in This Song

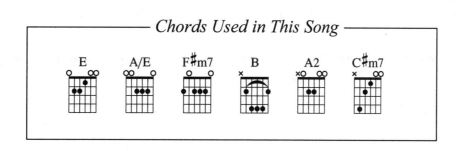

Yes And Amen

Words and Music by
MATT REDMAN, ROBERT MARVIN
and JOSIAH BELL

Slow Rock, ♩ = 75

Hear Your peo - ple say - ing yes,___ hear Your peo - ple say - ing yes___

___ to you.___ Yes to an - y - thing You ask,___

Yes to an - y - thing we're called___ to do.___

Hear Your peo - ple say a - men,___ Hear Your peo - ple say a - men___

228

men, to ev - 'ry - thing___ that's in Your heart___ Yes and a -
men, we're tak - ing up___ our cross for You.___ Give us the

men, to ev - 'ry - thing___ that You have planned.___ We
strength to take these dreams___ and fol - low through.___

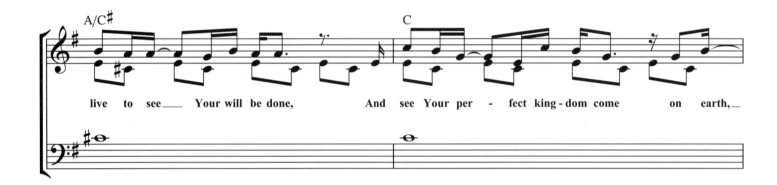

live to see___ Your will be done, And see Your per - fect king - dom come on earth,___

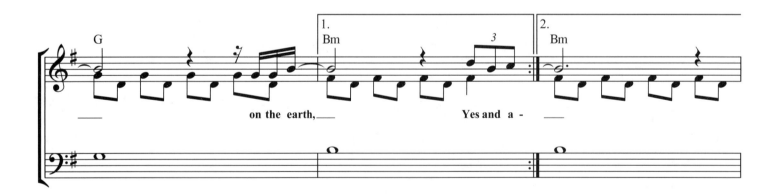

on the earth,___ Yes and a -

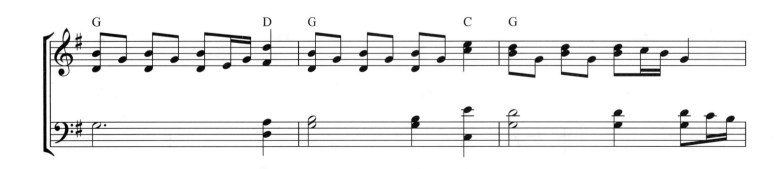

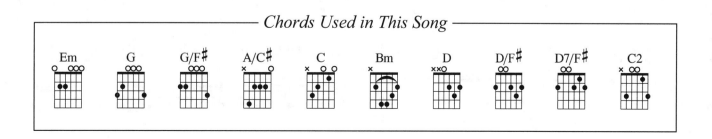

Chords Used in This Song

You Never Let Go

Words and Music by
MATT and BETH REDMAN

♩ = 76

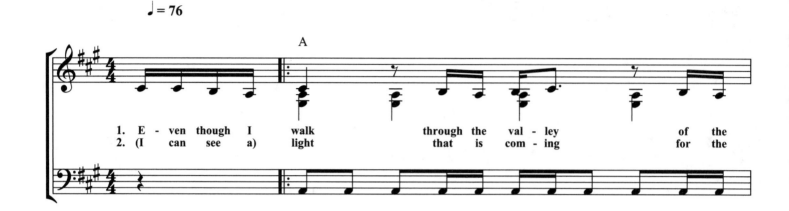

1. E - ven though I walk through the val - ley of the
2. (I can see a) light that is com - ing for the

shad - ow of death, Your per - fect love is cast - ing out fear,
heart that holds on, a glor - ious light be - yond all com - pare,

and e - ven when I'm caught in the mid - dle of the
and there will be an end to these trou - bles, but un -

storms of this life, I won't turn back, I know You are near.
til that day comes, we'll live to know You here on the earth.

234

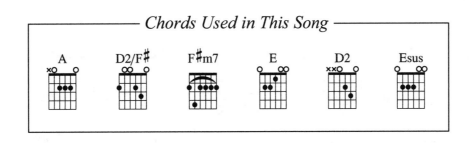

Chords Used in This Song

Your Glory Endures Forever

Words and Music by
CHARLIE HALL

Slow Rock, in two ♩. = 54

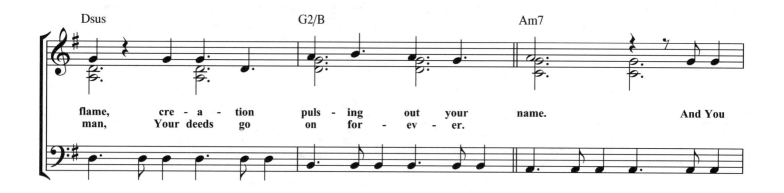

238

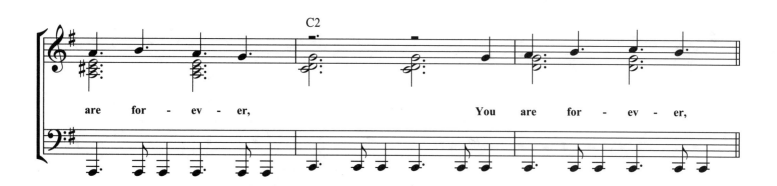

241

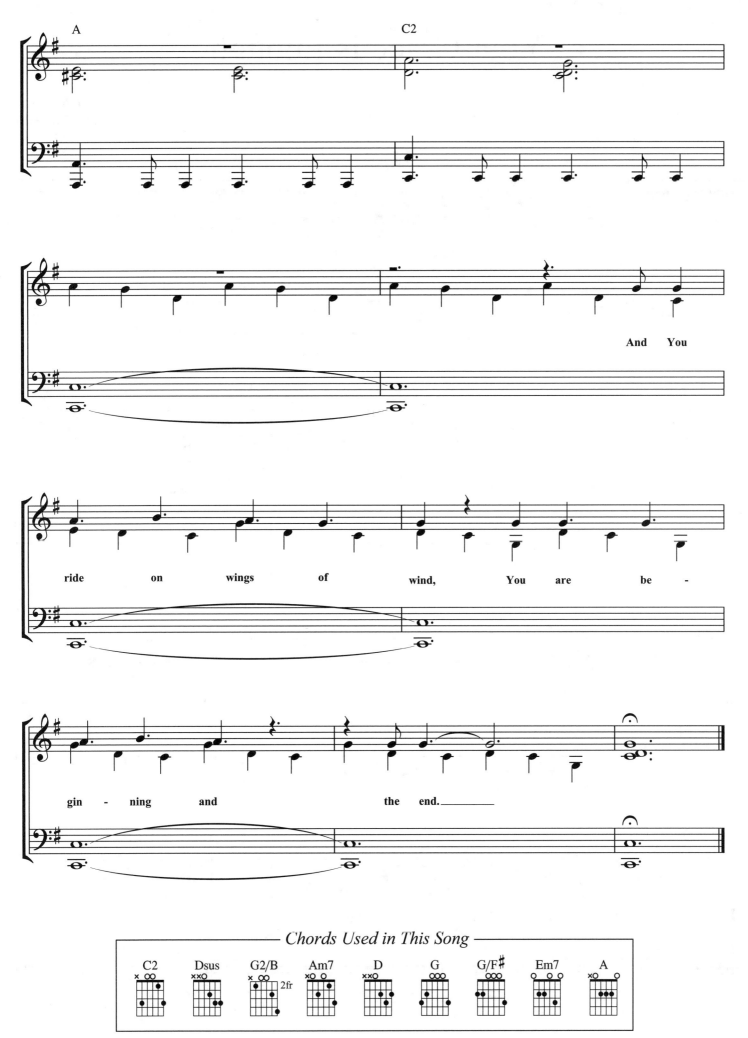

Chords Used in This Song

Your Grace Is Enough

Words and Music by
MATT MAHER

244

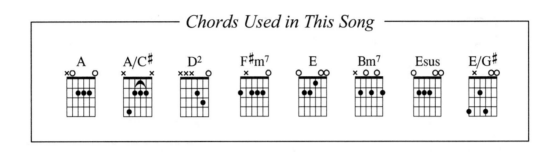

Chords Used in This Song

You Are My God
(Like A Whisper)

Words and Music by
BRENTON BROWN

Steady pace ♩ = 85

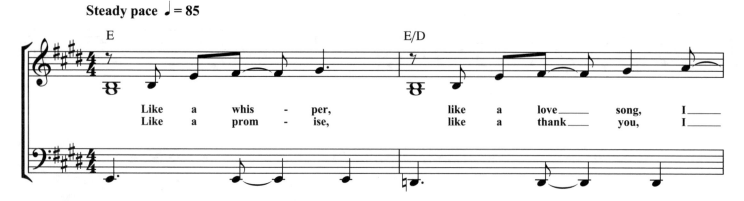

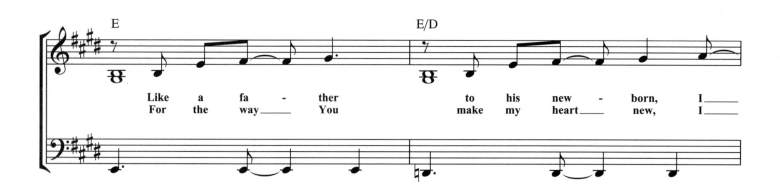

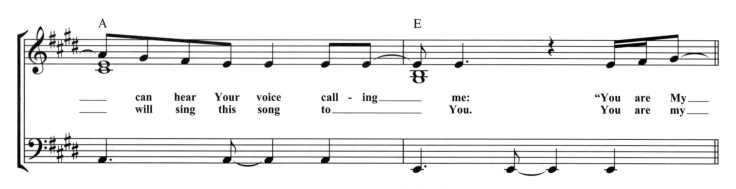

You, God, to be known as Yours. There is no

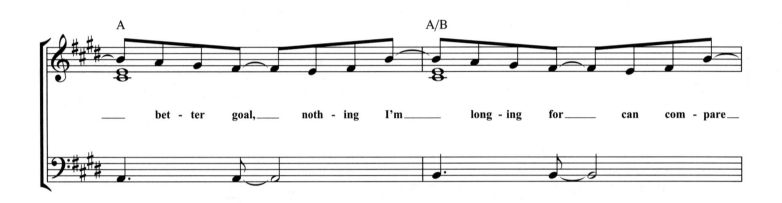

better goal, nothing I'm longing for can compare

D.S. al Fine

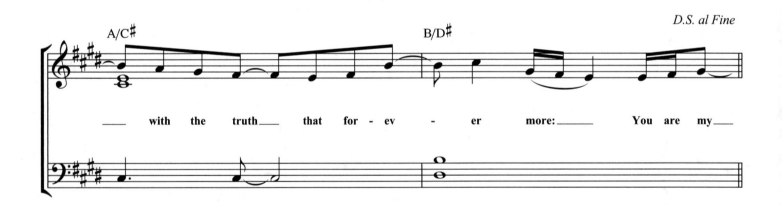

with the truth that for-ev-er more: You are my

Chords Used in This Song

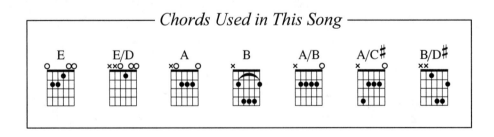

E   E/D   A   B   A/B   A/C#   B/D#

A Greater Song

PAUL BALOCHE and MATT REDMAN

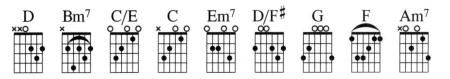

Sheet Music available at
WORSHIP TOGETHER.com

Scripture References

*Psalm 19:1
The heavens declare
the glory of God; the
skies proclaim the
work of His hands.*

*1 Chronicles 16:19
Sing to Him, sing
praise to Him, tell of
all His wonderful acts.*

Capo 2 (G)

VERSE 1:

D   Bm⁷   C/E   C
Who could imagine a mel - ody,

D   Bm⁷   C
True enough to tell of Your mer - cy?

D   Bm⁷   C/E C
Who could imagine a har - mony,

D   Bm⁷   C
Sweet enough to tell of Your love?

PRE-CHORUS :

          Em⁷
I see the heav - ens proclaiming You

  D/F♯
day   after day,

      G   C
And I know in my heart that there must be a way...

CHORUS 1:

      G   D/F♯
To sing a great - er song,

    Em⁷   C
A great - er song to You on the earth.

      G   D/F♯
To sing a great - er song,

    Em⁷   C
A great - er song to You on the earth.

VERSE 2:

D   Bm⁷   C/E   C
Who could imagine a sym - phony,

D   Bm⁷   C
Grand enough to tell of Your glo - ry?

D   Bm⁷   C/E   C
Our high - est praise but a fee - ble breath,

D   Bm⁷   C
A whisper of Your thunderous worth.

CONTINUED...

(REPEAT PRE-CHORUS)

(REPEAT CHORUS 1)

CHORUS 2:

G   D/F♯
Hallelujah, we want to lift You higher.

F   C
Hallelujah, we want to lift You higher.

G   D/F♯
Hallelujah, we want to lift You higher.

F   C
Hallelujah, we want to lift You higher.

Em⁷   F   Am⁷   F

Em⁷   C   Am⁷   F

(REPEAT PRE-CHORUS)

(REPEAT CHORUS 2 TWICE)

Theme(s):
Call To Worship
Adoration & Praise
Tempo:
96 bpm
Mid Up-Tempo
Played Key:
A
Vocal Range:

middle C

E - A

Similar Theme
Hosanna (Praise Is Rising)
Better Is One Day

Similar Tempo
All Over The World
Everlasting God

Similar Key
Grace
Hallelujah, Your Love Is Amazing

Scripture References

Psalm 34:3
*Glorify the Lord with
me; let us exalt His
name together.*

Psalm 99:5
*Exalt the lord our God
and worship at His
footstool; He is Holy.*

Adoration (Down In Adoration Falling)

THOMAS AQUINAS
Additional verse and chorus by MATT MAHER

C   Dm/C   F/C   G/C   G/B   Am⁷   Gsus   F   Dm⁷   G⁷   G   Em⁷   C/D   C/G   C/F   G/B   C/E   F/A

Theme(s):
Adoration & Praise

Tempo:
87 bpm
Mid Tempo

Played Key:
Db

Vocal Range:

middle C

Db - Db

Similar Theme
Center
Outrageous Grace

Similar Tempo
A Greater Song
Everything

Similar Key
It Is Well

Capo 1 (C)

VERSE:

C   Dm/C
Down in ado - ration falling,

F/C   Dm/C C
This great sacra - ment we hail;

      F/C
Over ancient forms departing,

       G/C
Newer rites of grace pre - vail;

C   Dm/C
Faith for all de - fects supplying

F/C   Dm/C C
Where the feeble senses fail.

PRE-CHORUS:

C
To the everlasting Father,

G/B
And the Son who reigns on high,

Am⁷
With the Spirit blest proceeding

Gsus
Forth from each eternally,

F
Be salvation, honor, blessing;

Dm⁷   G⁷ C
Might and endless majes - ty.

CHORUS 1:

(C)   F   G
 Jesus lamb of God, saving love for all,

      F   G
Lord of heaven and earth, Father's love for all;

 Am⁷ Em⁷ F
I bow to You.

CHORUS 2:

    G   F
Jesus lamb of God, saving love for all,

    G
Lord of heaven and earth,

 Am⁷ Em⁷ F (G   C) *Play first time only.*
I bow to You, (bow to You, I bow to You.)

CONTINUED...

INTERLUDE:

C   Dm⁷ C/D Am⁷

C/G   C/F   Dm⁷

BRIDGE:

C   G/B
Pour upon us Lord of Mercy,

Am⁷ Gsus F²
Spirit of Thy selfless love;

Am⁷   C/E
Make us of one true heart yearning

F   Am⁷ G/B
For the glory of Thy Son;

C   Dm⁷
Jesus, fire of justice blazing;

Am⁷   F G C
Gladdening light for - ever more.

(REPEAT CHORUS 1)

(REPEAT CHORUS 2 THREE TIMES)

ENDING:

     C   Dm⁷   C/E
I bow to You, bow to You, I bow to You,

    F/A G C
Bow to You, I bow to You.

F/C   C

All Over The World

MATT REDMAN and MARTIN SMITH

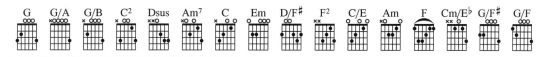

Sheet Music available at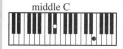

Capo 4 (G)

VERSE 1:

G   G/A   G/B
Even as the world   began the stars   they sang,
     C^2
And all   the Angels
Dsus   C^2 Dsus   C^2
Shouted for joy,   shouted for joy.
     G   G/A
And looking back through his - tory
       G/D   C^2
Your peo - ple they have al - ways had
    Dsus   C^2 Dsus   C^2
A song they must sing, a song they must sing.

PRE-CHORUS:

Am^7 G/D   C
We are the peo - ple of God.
Em   D/F$^\sharp$ F^2 C/E
We'll sing Your song   here on the earth.

CHORUS:

          G   Am
All over the world   Your song will resound.
          F   C
All over the world   Your praises ring out.
          G   Am
We're living to see   Your name and renown
          F   C
All over the world.

VERSE 2:

G   G/A
Young and old, near   and far,
     G/B   C^2
There's   a place for ev - ery heart
   Dsus   C^2 Dsus   C^2
To join in Your song,   join in Your song.
G   G/A
Every nation, tribe   and tongue
     G/B   C^2
Come   together, join   as one.
    Dsus   C^2 Dsus   C^2
Give glory to God, glory to God.

CONTINUED...

(REPEAT PRE-CHORUS)

(REPEAT CHORUS TWICE)

BRIDGE:

F
   Great is Your name and
       C/E   G
great   will be your song.
F
   Great is Your name and
       C/E   G
great   will be your song.
       F
We lift   up our hands and pray,
    C/E
We lift up our hands and pray
        Cm/E$^\flat$
For ho - ly is Your name.

G   G/F$^\sharp$ G/F   C/E

G   G/F$^\sharp$ G/F   C/E

(REPEAT CHORUS TWICE)

Scripture References

*Psalm 22:27
All the ends of the earth will remember and turn to the Lord, and all the families of the nations will bow down before Him.*

*Isaiah 55:12
You will go out in joy and be led forth in peace; the mountains and hills will burst into song before You, and all the trees of the field will clap their hands.*

Theme(s):
Church & Unity

Tempo:
96 bpm
Mid Up-Tempo

Played Key:
B

Vocal Range:

middle C

D# - E

Similar Theme
Consuming Fire
If We Are The Body

Similar Tempo
All Bow Down
Everything

Similar Key
Blessed Be Your Name
Nothing But The Blood

Scripture References

*Phillipian 4:19
And my God will meet all your needs according to His glorious riches in Christ Jesus.*

*John 3:5
"I tell you the truth, no one can enter the kingdom of God unless he is born of water and the Spirit."*

Theme(s):
Communion

Tempo:
122 bpm
Up Tempo

Played Key:
G

Vocal Range:

middle C

G - G

Similar Theme
Communion
Devotion

Similar Tempo
Name Above All Names
Wholly Yours

Similar Key
Revive Me
Your Love Goes On
Forever

All We Need

CHARLIE HALL

KEY OF (G)

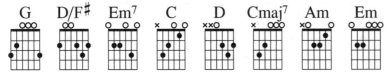

G   D/F♯   Em⁷   C   D   Cmaj⁷   Am   Em

CHORUS 1:

     G
And we have all we need in You,
D/F♯
   And all we need is You,
Em⁷   C
   All we need is You.

       G
Yeah, we have all we need in You,
D/F♯
   And all we need is You,
Em⁷   C
   All we need is You.

VERSE:

G
  Rich or poor, God, I want You more
D/F♯
   Than anything that glitters in this world;
Em⁷   C
   Be my all, all consuming fire.
G
  And you can have all my hands can hold,
D/F♯
   My heart, mind and strength and soul;
Em⁷   C
   Be my all, all consuming fire.

CHORUS 2:

       G
'Cause we have all we need in You,
D
   And all we need is You,
Em⁷   Cmaj⁷
   All we need is You.

      G
Yeah, we have all we need in You,
D
   And all we need is You,
Em⁷   Cmaj⁷
   All we need is You.

CONTINUED...

(REPEAT VERSE & CHORUS 2)

BRIDGE:

Am   Em   Am
           He's all we need.
Em   Am
  He's all we need.
Em   C
  'Cause You're all we need,

All we need, all we need.

(REPEAT CHORUS 2)

ENDING:

               G   D
All we need, all we need,
               Em⁷   Cmaj⁷
all we need   is You.

Almighty God

TIM HUGHES

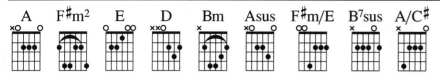

A   F#m²   E   D   Bm   Asus   F#m/E   B⁷sus   A/C#

Capo 1 (A)

VERSE 1:

A
    The rising Sun that fills the sky,
F#m²
      The starry host that lights the night,
E   D
    Reflecting Your glo - ry.

A
    The mountain heights, forever stand,
F#m²
      The rain that falls to soak the land,
E   D
    Respond to Your glo - ry.

CHORUS:

           A   E
Almighty God,   in every way,
           Bm   A   E
You are above   and be - yond understand - ing;
           A   E
If we did not praise,   the rocks would cry out,
           Bm   A*   E
Glorious God,   high a - bove understand - ing.
                   ***3rd time, play* A/C#**

CHORUS TAG:

    Asus   A   Asus   A
Yeah.

VERSE 2:

A
    The vast expanse of earth and sea,
F#m²
      Held by You in harmony,
E   D
    Speaks of Your glo - ry.

A
    All You've made, since time began,
F#m²
      Life itself; Your perfect plan,
E   D
    And it's all for Your glo - ry.

CONTINUED...

(REPEAT CHORUS)

BRIDGE:

F#m   F#m/E   A   D
    Crea - tion joins   as one   to sing
B⁷sus D   E
    "Glorious God,"
F#m   F#m/E   A   D
    So far   above   all earth - ly things.
B⁷sus   E

(REPEAT CHORUS TWICE)

ENDING:

         Asus   A   Asus   A
Yes Lord.

Sheet Music available at

Scripture References

Isaiah 40:13
Who has understood
the mind of the Lord,
or instructed him as
his counselor?

Psalm 19:1
The heavens declare
the glory of God; the
skies proclaim the
work of His hands.

Theme(s):
God's Attributes

Tempo:
88 bpm
Mid Tempo

Played Key:
Bb

Vocal Range:

middle C

Bb - F

Similar Theme
Everything
Filled With Your Glory

Similar Tempo
Beautiful Lord
Ready For You

Similar Key
God Of Wonders
Shout To The Lord

Sheet Music available at

WORSHIP TOGETHER.com

Scripture References

Psalm 27:8
My heart says of you,
"Seek His face!" Your
face, Lord, I will seek.

Revelation 1:17
When I saw Him, I fell
at his feet as though
dead. Then He placed
His right hand on me
and said "Do not be
afraid. I am the First
and the Last."

Theme(s):
Adoration & Praise

Tempo:
70 bpm
Slow Tempo

Played Key:
F

Vocal Range:

D - Bb

Similar Theme
Beautiful One
Yahweh

Similar Tempo
Give Us Clean Hands
The Heart Of Worship

Similar Key
Beautiful Savior (All My Days)
Unashamed

As We Seek Your Face
DAVE BILBROUGH

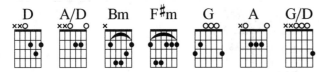

D   A/D   Bm   F#m   G   A   G/D

Capo 3 (D)

VERSE 1:

D A/D D
As we seek Your   face,

Bm   F#m   G
May we know Your   heart,

Bm A   Bm G
Feel Your pre - sence, ac - cep - tance,

D A/D D G/D   D
As we seek Your   face,

VERSE 2:

D A/D D
Move a - mong us   now,

Bm   F#m   G
Come re - veal Your   power,

Bm A   Bm G
Feel Your pres - ence, ac - cept - ance,

D A/D D G/D   D
Move a - mong us   now.

CONTINUED...

VERSE 3:

D A/D D
At Your feet we   fall,

Bm   F#m   G
Sovereign Lord,

Bm A Bm G
We cry "ho - ly, ho - ly,"

D A/D D G/D   D
At Your feet we   fall,

Awesome Is The Lord Most High

CHRIS TOMLIN, JESSE REEVES, CARY PIERCE and JON ABEL

KEY OF (A)

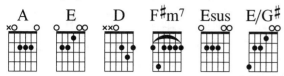

A   E   D   F#m⁷   Esus   E/G#

CONTINUED...

VERSE 1:

A   E
 Great are You, Lord, mighty in strength.

D
 You are faithful, and You will ever be.

A   E
 We will praise You all of our days,

D   F#m⁷
 It's for Your glory, we offer everything.

CHORUS 1:

(Esus)* A   ***1st & 2nd time only***
 Raise your hands all you nations,

    D
Shout to God all creation,

 F#m⁷   D
How awesome is the Lord most high.

VERSE 2:

A   E
 Where You send us, God we will go.

D
 You're the answer, we want the world to know.

A   E
 We will trust You when You call our name,

D   F#m⁷
 Where You lead us, we'll follow all the way.

(REPEAT CHORUS 1)

CHORUS 2:

      A
We will praise You together,

 E/G#
For now and forever.

 F#m⁷   D
How awesome is the Lord most high.

BRIDGE:

A   E
Hallelujah, hallelujah,

 F#m⁷   D
How awesome is the Lord most high.

A   E/G#
Hallelujah, hallelujah,

 F#m⁷   D
How awesome is the Lord most high.

(REPEAT CHORUS 1 & 2 TWICE)

A E/G# F#m⁷ D

Scripture References

Psalm 47:2
How awesome is the Lord Most High, the great King over all the earth.

Exodus 15:11
Who among the gods is like You, O Lord? Who is like you, majestic in holiness, awesome in glory, working wonders?

Sheet Music available at WORSHIP TOGETHER.com

Theme(s):
Adoration & Praise

Tempo:
138 bpm
Up Tempo

Played Key:
A

Vocal Range:

middle C

A - F

Similar Theme
Center
Son Of God

Similar Tempo
All We Need
See His Love

Similar Key
A Greater Song
Be Lifted High

Scripture References

*Lamentations 3:41
Let us lift up our
hearts and our hands
to God*

*Psalm 99:9
Exalt the Lord our
God and worship at
His holy mountain,
for the Lord our God
is holy*

Be Lifted High
LEELAND MOORING

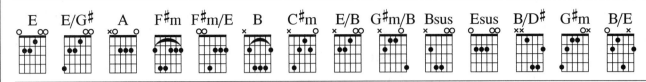

Theme(s):
Prayer & Renewal

Tempo:
76 bpm
Slow Mid-Tempo

Played Key:
Gb

Vocal Range:

middle C

Db - F

Similar Theme
Wholly Yours
As I Lift You Up

Similar Tempo
As We Seek Your Face
How Great Is Our God

Similar Key
As We Seek Your Face
A Greater Song

Capo 2 (E)

VERSE 1:

E   E/G#   A   E/G#
Sin and its ways   grow old,

F#m   F#m/E   B
All of my heart   turns to stone.

    C#m   E/B
And I'm left with no strength

  G#m/B B E/G#
to arise,

  F#m   Bsus B   Esus E
I need to be lift - ed high.

VERSE 2:

E   E/G#   A   E/G#
Sin and its ways   lead to pain,

F#m   F#m/E   B
Left here with hurt   and shame.

    C#m   E/B   B E/G#
So no longer will I leave Your side,

    F#m Bsus B   Esus E
Jesus, You be lift - ed high.

CHORUS:

A   E/G# A   E/G#
You be lifted high,   You be lifted high,

F#m F#m/E B/D#
You be lifted high   in my life,

C#m G#m   A
  oh   God.

    F#m   F#m/E   B/D#
And I fall to my knees   so it's You

      C#m G#m A
that they see,   not   I,

    F#m Bsus B   Esus E
Jesus, You be lift - ed high.

CONTINUED...

VERSE 3:

     E   E/G#
And even now that I'm in - side

      A   E/G#
Your hands,

     F#m   F#m/E   B
Help me not to grow pride - ful again.

    C#m   E/B   G#m/B B E/G#
Don't let me forsake   sac - rifice,

    F#m Bsus B   Esus E
Jesus, You be lift - ed high.

VERSE 4:

     E   E/G#
And if I'm blessed with the rich - es

      A   E/G#
of kings,

     F#m   F#m/E   B
How could I ever think that   it was me?

    C#m   E/B
For You brought me from dark - ness

G#m/B B E/G#
to light,

    F#m Bsus B   Esus E
Jesus, You be lift - ed high.

(REPEAT CHORUS TWICE)

    F#m   Bsus B B/E E B/E E
Jesus, You be lift - ed high.

Beautiful Lord
LEELAND MOORING and MARC BYRD

Sheet Music available at

KEY OF (C)

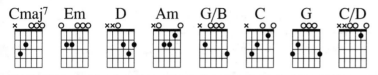

Cmaj⁷   Em   D   Am   G/B   C   G   C/D

Scripture References

*Ephesians 2:4-6
But because of His
great love for us, God,
who is rich in mercy,
made us alive with
Christ even when we
were dead in trans-
gressions - it is by
grace you have been
saved.*

CONTINUED...

VERSE 1:

Cmaj⁷   Em   D
When the storm is raging all around me,
    Cmaj⁷   Em   D
You are the peace that calms my troubled sea,
    Cmaj⁷   Em   D
When the cares of this world darken my day,
        Cmaj⁷
You are the light that shines
    Em   D
And shows me the way.

PRE-CHORUS:

    Am   G/B   C
Oh the beauty of Your majesty,
    Am   G/B   C
On the cross You showed Your love for me.

CHORUS:

        Cmaj⁷   Em   D
Beautiful Lord,   awe - some and mighty,
    Cmaj⁷   Em   D
I'm captured by this love I see.
        Cmaj⁷   Em   D
Beautiful Lord,   ten - der and holy,
    Cmaj⁷   Em   D
Your mercy brings me to my knees.
            Am   G/B   C
It's Your mer   -   cy that has made me free,

TAG:

        Cmaj⁷   Em   D
Beautiful Lord.

Cmaj⁷   Em   D

VERSE 2:

        Cmaj⁷   Em   D
When my sin is all that I can see,
            Cmaj⁷   Em   D
Your grace re - mains the shelter that I seek,
            Cmaj⁷   Em   D
And when my weakness is all I can give,
        Cmaj⁷   Em   D
Your gentle Spirit gives me strength again.

(REPEAT PRE-CHORUS & CHORUS)

BRIDGE:

            G   D
And I am lifted by Your love to sing,
        Am   G/B   C
It's Your mercy that has made me free,
            G   D
And I am lifted by Your love to sing,
        Am   G/B   C
It's Your mercy that has made me free.
C/D   D

(REPEAT PRE-CHORUS, CHORUS & TAG)

ENDING:

                Cmaj⁷   Em   D
You're beautiful,   my Lord.
                Cmaj⁷   Em   D
You're beautiful,   my Lord.
                Cmaj⁷   Em   D
You're beautiful.

Theme(s):
Grace & Mercy

Tempo:
80 bpm
Mid Tempo

Played Key:
C

Vocal Range:

middle C

D - B

Similar Theme
Above All
Take Us To The River

Similar Tempo
Enter In
Take My Life

Similar Key
I Believe In You
The Wonderful Cross

Sheet Music available at

WORSHIP TOGETHER.com

Scripture References

*Luke 14:15
When one of those
at the table with him
heard this, he said
to Jesus, "Blessed is
the man who will eat
at the feast in the
kingdom of God"*

Carried To The Table

LEELAND MOORING, MARC BYRD and STEVE HINDALONG

KEY OF (D)

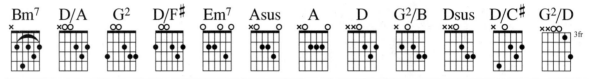

Bm⁷ D/A G² D/F# Em⁷ Asus A D G²/B Dsus D/C# G²/D

Theme(s):
Love

Tempo:
68 bpm
Slow Mid - Tempo

Played Key:
D

Vocal Range:

A - G

Similar Theme
See His Love
You Never Let Go

Similar Tempo
Be Lifted High
Strong Tower

Similar Key
The Heart Of Worship
Strong Tower

VERSE 1:

Bm⁷   D/A
Wounded and forsaken,
        G²   A
I was shattered by the fall,
Bm⁷   D/A
Broken and forgotten,
        G²   D/F#
feeling lost and all alone.
Em⁷
Summoned by the King
        Asus   A
into   the master's courts,
Em⁷
Lifted by the Savior
        Asus   A
and cradled in His arms.

CHORUS OPENING 1:

        D/F#   G²   D/F#
I was carried to the ta - ble,

CHORUS:

Em⁷   A   D   D/C#
     seated where I don't belong,
G²/B   D/F#   G²   D/F#
     Carried to the ta - ble,
Em⁷   A   D
     swept a - way by His love.
        Em⁷   Dsus   Asus
And I don't see my bro - kenness any - more,
A   Em⁷   Dsus   Asus
   When I'm seated at the ta - ble of the Lord.
        A   D/F#   G²   G²/F#
I'm carried to the ta - ble,
Em⁷   A   (D   D/C#)*
   the table of the Lord.
                        1st time only

VERSE 2:

Bm⁷   D/A
Fighting thoughts of fear,
        G²   A
wond'ring why He called my name,
        Bm⁷   D/A
Am I good enough to share this cup,
        G²   D/F#
this world has left me lame.

(CONTINUED...)

Em⁷
Even in my weakness,
        Asus   A
the Savior called my name.
Em⁷
In His Holy presence,
        Asus   A
I'm healed and una - shamed.

CHORUS OPENING 2:

        D/F#   G²   D/F#
As I'm carried to the ta - ble,

(REPEAT CHORUS)

INTERLUDE 1:

G²/B   D/A   G²/B   D/A

G²/B   D/A   Em⁷

CHORUS OPENING 3:

        A   D/F#   G²
I'm carried to the ta - ble

(REPEAT CHORUS)

INTERLUDE 2:

G²/D   D   G²/D   D

G²/D   D   Em⁷   A

ENDING:

G²/D   D
        You carried me   my God,
G²/D   D
        You carried me.
G²/D   D
        You carried me   my God,
Em⁷   A
        You carried me.

(REPEAT ENDING FIVE TIMES AND FADE)

Center

CHARLIE HALL and MATT REDMAN

KEY OF (E)

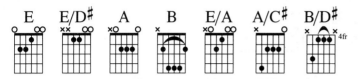

Sheet Music available at
WORSHIP TOGETHER.com

Scripture References

*Romans 11:36
For from Him and
through Him and to
Him are all things.
to Him be the glory
forever! Amen.*

CHORUS:

         E   E/D♯
Oh, Christ, be the cen - ter of our lives,
A
  Be the place we fix our eyes,
E   E/D♯   A
  Be the cen - ter of our lives.

VERSE:

                E
And You're the center of the universe,
B   A
Everything was made in You,   Jesus.
E
Breath of every living thing,
B   A
Everyone was made for You.

PRE-CHORUS 1:

      E/A   E   E/A   B
You hold ev - 'ry-thing to - geth - er,
      A/C♯   E   E/A   B
You hold ev - 'ry-thing to - geth - er.

(REPEAT CHORUS TWICE)

(REPEAT VERSE)

PRE-CHORUS 2:

      E/A   E   E/A   B
You hold ev - 'ry-thing to - geth - er,
      A/C♯   E   E/A   B/D♯
You hold ev - 'ry-thing to - geth - er.
      E/A   E   E/A   B
You hold ev - 'ry-thing to - geth - er,
      A/C♯   E   E/A   B
You hold ev - 'ry-thing to - geth - er.

CONTINUED...

(REPEAT CHORUS)

BRIDGE:

E   E/D♯
We lift our eyes to heav - en,
        A
And we wrap our lives around Your life,
E   E/D♯   A
We lift our eyes to heav - en, to You.

(REPEAT BRIDGE & CHORUS)

INSTRUMENTAL:

E   E/D♯   A
E   E/D♯   A

(REPEAT BRIDGE TWICE)

ENDING:

    E   E/D♯   A
And turn your eyes upon Jesus,
                  *(B)
And look full in His wonderful face.
   (E)   (A)
And the things of earth will grow strangely dim,
   (E)   (A) (E)
In the light of His glory and grace.

*Chords in parentheses reflect implied harmony.

Theme(s):
Adoration & Praise

Tempo:
112 bpm
Mid Up-Tempo

Played Key:
E

Vocal Range:

middle C

B - B

Similar Theme
Bless The Lord
Dancing Generation

Similar Tempo
Everlasting God
Famous One

Similar Key
Our Love Is Loud
Sing To The King

Scripture References

John 7:37-38
[37]On the last and greatest day of the Feast, Jesus stood and said in a loud voice, "If anyone is thirsty, let him come to me and drink. [38]Whoever believes in me, as the Scripture has said, streams of living water will flow from within him."

Matthew 11:28
"Come to me, all you who are weary and burdened, and I will give you rest."

Theme(s):
Prayer & Renewal

Tempo:
138 bpm
Up Tempo

Played Key:
Bb

Vocal Range:

D - F

Similar Theme
Be Lifted High
Wholly Yours

Similar Tempo
Blessed Be Your Name
Holy Moment

Similar Key
Here Is Our King
A Greater Song

Closer

CHARLIE HALL, KENDALL COMBES, DUSTIN RAGLAND and BRIAN BERGMAN

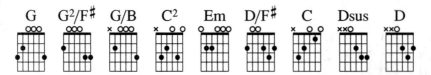

G   G^2/F#   G/B   C^2 Em   D/F#   C   Dsus   D

Capo 3 (G)

VERSE:

G   G^2/F#   G/B   C^2
Beautiful are the words   spoken to me,

G   G^2/F#   G/B   C^2

G   G^2/F#   G/B   C^2
Beautiful is the one   who is   speaking.

G   G^2/F#   G/B   C^2

(REPEAT VERSE)

CHORUS 1:

G   G^2/F#   G/B   C^2
Come in close,

G   G^2/F#   G/B   C^2
come in close   and speak,

G   G^2/F#   G/B   C^2
Come in close,   come closer to me.

G   G^2/F#   G/B   C^2

(REPEAT VERSE)

(REPEAT CHORUS 1)

INTERLUDE:

G   G^2/F#   G/B   C^2

(CONTINUED...)

BRIDGE:

G   G^2/F#
And the power of Your words

G/B   C^2
Are filled with grace and mercy.

G   G^2/F#   G/B   C^2
Let them fall on my ears and break my stony heart

(REPEAT BRIDGE)

CHORUS 2:

Em   D/F#   G   C
Come in close,   come in close and speak,

Em   Dsus   C^2
Come in close,   come closer to me.

Dsus   D   *Sung 2nd time only*
(Come closer to me.)*

(REPEAT CHORUS 2)

(REPEAT INTERLUDE)

(REPEAT BRIDGE TWICE)

(REPEAT CHORUS TWICE)

ENDING:

G

Communion

MAC POWELL and THIRD DAY

Sheet Music
WORSHIP TOGE...

Scripture Refere...

*Matthew 5:6
Blessed are those who
hunger and thirst for
righteousness, for they
will be filled.*

KEY OF (D)

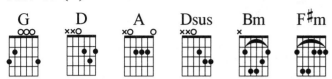

CHORUS:

        G   D
This is the body, this is the blood

        A   D Dsus D
Broken and poured out, for all of us

        G   Bm
In this communion, we share in His love

        A G   D
This is the body   This is the blood

VERSE 1:

Bm   G   D
    I will remember, everything Lord

           Dsus
That you've done for me

Bm   G   D
    I won't take for granted, the sacrifice

         A
That set me free

PRECHORUS:

F#m   G
    I hunger and thirst for Your love

F#m   A
    Come fill me today   *(REPEAT CHORUS)*

INSTRUMETAL TAG:

Bm G D Dsus Bm G D A

BRIDGE:

F#m   G   F#m   G
    We hunger and thirst for Your love   and Your righteousness

F#m   G   F#m   A
    We long for Your presense here Lord be with us again *(REPEAT CHORUS 2x)*

TAG:

        A G   D
This is the body   This is the blood *(REPEAT 2x)*

Theme(s):
Communion

Tempo:
dotted quarter 50 bpm
Slow Tempo

Played Key:
D

Vocal Range:

middle C

D - E

Similar Theme
Breathe
Offering

Similar Tempo
Gifted Response
Wonderful King

Similar Key
How Majestic Is Your
Name
Prepare The Way

Theme(s):
Jesus

Tempo:
152 bpm
Up Tempo

Played Key:
Ab

Vocal Range:

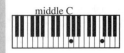

middle C

G - F

Similar Theme
Because Of You
See His Love

Similar Tempo
All We Need
See His Love

Similar Key
Awesome Is The Lord
Most High
Closer

Declare Victory (Canticle Of Zechariah)

MATT MAHER and TAM LE

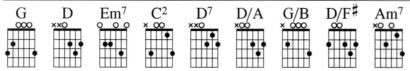

G   D   Em⁷   C²   D⁷   D/A   G/B   D/F♯   Am⁷

Capo 1 (G)

VERSE 1:

G   D
  The dawn breaks   upon us
Em⁷   C²
   With tender   compassion,
G   D
  To shine in   the darkness
Em⁷   C²
   And we become   Your righteousness.

VERSE 2:

G   D
  Your promise   if mercy
Em⁷   C²   D⁷
   Now made true   on Calva - ry,
G   D/A
  Our ransom   has been paid
Em⁷   C²   D⁷
   And now we   prepare the   way.

PRE-CHORUS 1:

(C²   G/B   Em⁷   D)   D/F♯   G
                                        De - clare   victory;
(C²   G/B   Em⁷   D)   G/B   C²
                                    You   set us free.

CHORUS:

G
  For from You and through You
C²
  And for You are all things,
Em⁷   C²
   To You be all glory,   all honor, all blessing.
G
  For from You and through You
C²
  And for You are all things,
Em⁷   C²
   To You be all glory,   all honor, all blessing.

CONTINUED...

VERSE 3:

G   D
  From all sin   and evil,
Em⁷   C²   D⁷
   From the snares   of the de - vil,
G   D/A
  From Your wrath,   from our death,
Em⁷
   From a doubtful heart
C²   D⁷
   That chokes on human   breath.

PRE-CHORUS 2:

(C²   G/B   Em⁷   D)   D/F♯   G
                                        You de - liver me,
(C²   G/B   Em⁷   D)   G/B   C²
                                    You   set us free.

(REPEAT CHORUS)

BRIDGE:

G
Halleluiah, Halleluiah.
                Am⁷   G/B   C²
Halle - luiah,   Halle - luiah.

(REPEAT PRE-CHORUS 1 & CHORUS)

ENDING:

G   C²   Em⁷   C²
Halle - luiah,   Halle - luiah.
G   C²   Em⁷   D/F♯   C²   G
Halle - luiah,   Hal - le - luiah.

Everlasting God

BRENTON BROWN and KEN RILEY

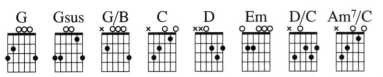

G   Gsus   G/B   C   D   Em   D/C   Am⁷/C

Capo 3 (G)   *All chords in parentheses are optional*

VERSE:

G   (Gsus)   G
   Strength will rise as we wait up - on the Lord,
    (Gsus)   G
We will wait up - on the Lord,
    (Gsus)   G
We will wait up - on the Lord.
G   (Gsus)   G
   Strength will rise as we wait up - on the Lord,
    (Gsus)   G
We will wait up - on the Lord,
    (Gsus)   G
We will wait up - on the Lord.

PRE-CHORUS:

(G/B)   C   (G/B   C   D)   Em   D
 Our   God, You   reign for - ev - er.
(G/B)   C   (G/B   C   D)   Em   D
 Our   hope, our   strong De - liv - 'rer.

CHORUS:

G   C
   You are the everlasting God,   the everlasting God.
Em   C   (D/C   C   Am⁷/C)
    You do not faint, You won't grow wea - ry.
G
   You're the defender of the weak,
C
   You comfort those in need.
Em   C   (D/C   C   Am⁷/C)
    You lift us up on wings like   eagles.

CONTINUED...

(REPEAT VERSE, PRE-CHORUS & CHORUS)

INSTRUMENTAL 1:

(G/B)   C   (G/B   C   D)   Em   D

(G/B)   C   (G/B   C   D)   Em   D

(REPEAT PRE-CHORUS & CHORUS)

INSTRUMENTAL 2:

G   (Gsus)   G   (Gsus)   G   (Gsus)   G

(REPEAT CHORUS)

G

Sheet Music
WORSHIP TOG...

Scripture Refer...

Isaiah 40:28-31
Do you not know?
Have you not heard?
The Lord is the
everlasting God, the
Creator of the ends of
the earth. He will not
grow tired or weary,
and his understanding
no one can fathom.
He gives strength
to the weary and
increases the power
of the weak. Even
youths grow tired and
weary, and young men
stumble and fall; but
those who hope in the
Lord will renew their
strength. They will
soar on wings like
eagles; they will run
and not grow weary,
they will walk and not
be faint.

Theme(s):
Peace & Hope

Tempo:
108 bpm
Mid Up-Tempo

Played Key:
Bb

Vocal Range:

middle C

Bb - D

Similar Theme
I Can Only Imagine
What A Friend I've
Found

Similar Tempo
All Bow Down
Jesus Lord Of Heaven

Similar Key
Here Is Our King
O Praise Him

Everything

TIM HUGHES

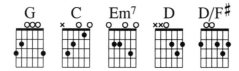

Capo 4 (G)

VERSE 1:

G   C
God in my liv - ing, there in my breath - ing.

Em⁷   D
God in my wak - ing, God in my sleep - ing.

G   C
God in my rest - ing, there in my work - ing.

Em⁷   D
God in my think - ing, God in my speak - ing.

CHORUS:

      C   D   Em⁷
Be my ev'ry - thing, be my ev'ry - thing.
(You are) *8th time*
(Jesus) *last time*

D   C   D   G
 Be my ev'ry - thing, be my ev'ry - thing.

VERSE 2:

     G   C
God in my hop - ing, there in my dream - ing.

    Em⁷   D
God in my watch - ing, God in my wait - ing.

     G   C
God in my laugh - ing, there in my weep - ing.

    Em⁷   D
God in my hurt - ing, God in my heal - ing.

(REPEAT CHORUS)

CONTINUED...

BRIDGE:

C   D
 Christ in me, Christ in me,

Em⁷
   Christ in me the hope of glory,

C   D   Em⁷
 You are ev'rything.

C   D
 Christ in me, Christ in me,

Em⁷
   Christ in me the hope of glory,

C D   Em⁷   D/F♯
 Be my ev'ry - thing.

(REPEAT CHORUS TWICE)

(REPEAT VERSE 2)

(REPEAT CHORUS FIVE TIMES)

Theme(s):
God's Attributes

Tempo:
104 bpm
Mid Up-Tempo

Played Key:
B

Vocal Range:

middle C

D# - G#

Similar Theme
Almighty God
O Sacred King

Similar Tempo
A Greater Song
Awesome Is The Lord
Most High

Similar Key
All Over The World
Be Lifted High

Everything Glorious

DAVID CROWDER

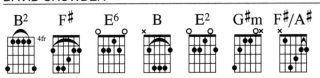

B²   F♯   E⁶   B   E²   G♯m   F♯/A♯

Capo 2 (B)

Verse 1:

B²   F♯   E⁶
    The day   is bright - er here with You,

B²   F♯   E⁶
    The night   is light - er than its hue,

B²   F♯   E⁶
    Would lead   me to believe,

B²   F♯   E⁶
    Which leads   me to believe:

CHORUS:

B   F♯   E²
You make ev - 'rything glo - rious,

B   F♯   E²
You make ev - 'rything glo - rious,

B   F♯   E²
You make ev - 'rything glo - rious,

         B   F♯   E²
And I am Yours,

CHORUS TAG:

           B²   F♯   E⁶
What does that make me?

B²   F♯   E⁶

VERSE 2:

B²   F♯   E⁶
    My eyes   are small   but they have seen,

B²   F♯   E⁶
    The beau - ty of   enormous things,

B²   F♯   E⁶
    Which leads   me to believe,

B²   F♯   E⁶
    There's light   e - nough to see that:

CONTINUED...

(REPEAT CHORUS)

BRIDGE:

G♯m   F♯/A♯
    From glory   to glory,

B   F♯
    You are glorious,   You are glorious,

E²   F♯/A♯
    From glory   to glory,

B   F♯
    You are glorious,   You are glorious,

E²
    Which leads me to believe, why I can believe.

(REPEAT CHORUS TWICE)

REFRAIN:

B   F♯   E²
    From glo - ry   to glory,

B   F♯   E²
    From glo - ry   to glory,

B   F♯   E²
    You are glo - rious,   You are glorious,

B   F♯   E²
    You are glo - rious,   You are glorious,

B²   F♯   E⁶   B²   F♯   E⁶

B²   F♯   E⁶   B²   F♯   E⁶

(REPEAT CHORUS)

B²   F♯   E⁶   B

Sheet Music available at
WORSHIP TOGETHER.com

Scripture References

Hebrews 1:3
The Son is the radiance of god's glory and the exact representation of his being, sustaining all things by his powerful word. After he had provided purification for sins, he sat down at the right hand of the Majesty in heaven.

Theme(s):
Jesus

Tempo:
92 bpm
Mid Tempo

Played Key:
Db

Vocal Range:

middle C

Db - F

Similar Theme
Declare Victory
See His Love

Similar Tempo
Almighty God
Resurrection Hymn

Similar Key
Nothing But The Blood
You Are My Joy

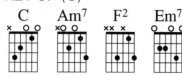
Scripture References

Matthew 16:24
The Jesus said to his disciples, "If anyone would come after me, he must deny himself and take up his cross and follow me."

Mark 2:17
On hearing this, Jesus said to them, "It is not the healthy who need a doctor, but the sick. I have not come to call the righteous, but sinners."

Theme(s):
Jesus

Tempo:
84 bpm
Mid Tempo

Played Key:
C

Vocal Range:

middle C

A - E

Similar Theme
Declare Victory
Everything Glorious

Similar Tempo
Almighty God
Everything Glorious

Similar Key
Beautiful Lord
He Reigns

Give Me Jesus
JEREMY CAMP

KEY OF (C)

C   Am^7 F^2 Em^7

VERSE 1:

       C   Am^7
In the morn - ing when I   rise,

        F^2 C
In the morn - ing when I rise,

        Am^7 F^2
In the morn - ing when I   rise,

          C
Give me Je - sus.

CHORUS:

       Em^7 Am^7
Give me Jesus,

       F^2 C
Give me Jesus,

         Am^7 F^2
You can have   all this world,

CHORUS TAG:

          C
Just give me Je - sus.

VERSE 2:

C   Am^7
When I am alone,

F^2 C
When I am alone,

Am^7 F^2
When I am alone,

        C
Give me Je - sus.

(REPEAT CHORUS & CHORUS TAG)

CONTINUED...

INTERLUDE:

C Am^7 F^2 C
        Jesus,

    Am^7 F^2 C
Give   me Jesus.

VERSE 3:

C   Am^7
When I come to die,

F^2 C
When I come to die,

Am^7 F^2
When I come to die,

        C
Give me Je - sus.

(REPEAT CHORUS & CHORUS TAG)

(REPEAT CHORUS)

ENDING:

        Am^7 F^2
You can have   all this world,

        Am^7 F^2
You can have   all this world,

        C
Just give me Je - sus.

Am^7 F C Am^7 F C

      Am^7 F^2 C
Jesus.

Give You Glory

JEREMY CAMP

KEY OF (D)

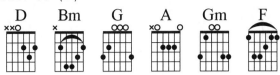

Sheet Music available at
WORSHIP **TOGETHER**.com

Scripture References

*Revelations 14:7
He said in a loud voice, "Fear God and give him glory, because the hour of his judgement has come. Worship him who made the heavens, the earth, the sea and the springs of water."*

*Psalm 113:5
Who is like the Lord our God, the One who sits enthroned on high.*

Theme(s):
Adoration & Praise

Tempo:
132 bpm
Up Tempo

Played Key:
D

Vocal Range:

B - E

Similar Theme
Adoration
Center

Similar Tempo
Beautiful One
Joy Is In This Place

Similar Key
Dancing Generation
The Answer

VERSE 1:

D
We have raised a thousand voices,

Bm
Just to lift Your holy name,

G
And we will raise thousands more,

A
To sing of Your beauty in this place.

D
None can even fathom,

Bm
No, not one define Your worth,

G
As we marvel in Your presence

A
To the ends of the earth.

CHORUS:

D
We give You glory,

Bm
Lifting up our hands and singing Holy,

G
You alone are worthy,

Gm
We just want to touch   Your heart Lord,

Touch Your heart.

D   Bm
Glory, lifting up our voice and singing Holy,

G
You alone are worthy,

Gm
We just want to touch   Your heart Lord,

Touch Your heart.

CONTINUED...

VERSE 2:

D
As we fall down before You,

Bm
With our willing hearts we seek,

G
In the greatness of Your glory,

A
It's so hard to even speak.

D
There is nothing we can offer,

Bm
No, nothing can repay,

G
So we give You all our praises,

A
And lift our voice to sing.

(REPEAT CHORUS)

BRIDGE:

Bm   G   A
Our hope is drenched in You,

Bm   G   A
Our faith has been re - newed.

Bm   G   A
We trust in Your every word,

F   G   A
Nothing else can even measure up to You.

(REPEAT CHORUS THREE TIMES)

D

Scripture References

Isaiah 30:18
Yet the Lord longs to
be gracious to you;
he rises to show you
compassion. For the
Lord is a God of
justice. Blessed are
all who wait for him!
.

God Of Justice

TIM HUGHES

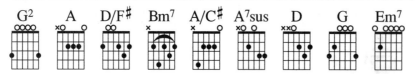

G²   A   D/F♯   Bm⁷   A/C♯   A⁷sus   D   G   Em⁷

Capo 3 (D)

VERSE 1:

G²   A   D/F♯
   God of jus - tice, Savior to all.

G²   A   D/F♯
   Came to res - cue the weak and the poor.

G²   A   D/F♯
   Chose to serve   and not   be served.

G²   A   D/F♯

PRE-CHORUS 1:

Bm⁷   A/C♯
Jesus, You have called us,

G²   A⁷sus
Freely we've received, now freely we will   give.

CHORUS:

     D   A/C♯
We must go, live to feed the hungry,

        Bm⁷   G²
Stand beside the broken, we must go.

     D   A/C♯
Stepping forward, keep us from just singing,

       Bm⁷   G²
Move us into action, we must go.

VERSE 2:

G²   A   D/F♯
   To act just - ly, every day.

G²   A   D/F♯
   Loving mer - cy, in every way.

G²   A   D/F♯
   Walking humb - ly, be - fore You, God.

G²   A   D/F♯

CONTINUED...

PRE-CHORUS 2:

       Bm⁷   A/C♯
You have shown us what You require,

G²   A⁷sus
Freely we've received, now freely we will   give.

(REPEAT CHORUS TWICE)

CHANNEL:

G²
   Fill us up and send us out,

A   D/F♯
Fill us up and send us out,

G²
   Fill us up and send us out Lord.

A   D/F♯

(REPEAT CHANNEL THREE TIMES)

(REPEAT CHORUS TWICE)

ENDING:

G
   As we worship you through song,

           D   Em⁷
We re - mind ourselves that we must go.

G
   As we seek your face,

           D   Em⁷   G
We re - mind ourselves of a broken world.

Theme(s):
Missions

Tempo:
78 bpm
Mid Tempo

Played Key:
F

Vocal Range:

middle C

C - F

Similar Theme
Marvelous Light
Shout To The North

Similar Tempo
The Everlasting
Who Is There Like You

Similar Key
As We Seek Your Face
In The Cross Alone I
Glory

Sheet Music available at
WORSHIP **TOGETHER** .com

Great God Of Wonders

ANDY BROMLEY

KEY OF (E)

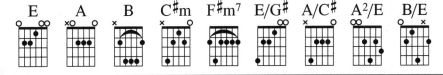

E   A   B   C#m   F#m⁷   E/G#   A/C#   A²/E   B/E

Scripture References

Psalm 40:5
Many, O Lord my God, are the wonders you have done. The things you planned for us no one can recount to you; were I to speak and tell of them, they would be too many to declare.

Psalm 113:3
From the rising of the sun to the place where it sets, the name of the Lord is to be praised.

CONTINUED...

VERSE:

E
Great God of wonders, Great God in power,

   A
The heavens are declaring glories of Your name,

B A   E
     Glories of Your name.

Great God of Zion, Great God in beauty,

   A
The nations are gathering to worship at Your feet,

B A   E
     To worship at Your feet.

PRE-CHORUS:

B   C#m
   From the rising to the setting sun,

   A
Your name   will be praised.

F#m⁷
God above all gods,

E/G#
King above all kings,

A   B
Lord of heaven and earth.

CHORUS 1:

        E   A   B
We give to You praise, praise, praise.

A/C#
    Give You

E   A   B   (E) *1st time only*
 praise, praise, praise.

(REPEAT VERSES)

(REPEAT PRE-CHORUS)

(REAPET CHRUS)

BRIDGE:

          E   B
You are the   great God a - bove all gods,

          A   B
You are the   great King a - bove all kings

          E   B
You are the   great Lord of heaven and earth,

        A   B
We give You praise.

(REPEAT BRIDGE)

CHORUS 2:

        E   A²/E   B/E
We give You praise,   praise,   praise.

        E   A²/E   B
We give You praise,   praise,   praise.

(REPEAT CHORUS 1)

E   A   B   A/C#

ENDING:

          B
Only Lord, worthy all our praise, Lord Jesus.

          A   E
Hallelujah, Lord, Hallelu.

Theme(s):
Adoration & Praise

Tempo:
104 bpm
Mid Up-Tempo

Played Key:
E

Vocal Range:

middle C

E - E

Similar Theme
Beautiful One
Give You Glory

Similar Tempo
Center
Overflow

Similar Key
Come, Now Is The Time
To Worship
Sing To The King

Scripture References

*Psalm 89:1
I will sing of the Lord's great love forever; with my mouth I will make your faithfulness known through all generations.*

*James 4:8
Come near to God and He will come near to you. Wash your hands, you sinners, and purify your hearts, you double-minded.*

Theme(s):
Adoration & Praise

Tempo:
100 bpm
Mid Up-Tempo

Played Key:
A

Vocal Range:

middle C

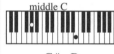

G# - B

Similar Theme
Everlasting God
Hear Our Song

Similar Tempo
Center
Everlasting God

Similar Key
Empty Me
Mighty Is The Power Of
The Cross

Hallelujah God Is Near

ROBBIE SEAY, RYAN OWENS, DAN HAMILTON and TAYLOR JOHNSON

KEY OF (A)

A^7 G C F^2 Am F G^7

CONTINUED...

VERSE 1:

A^7
   God's resplendent glory full

G
   On display for all to see.

A^7
   God creator, God of hope,

G A^7
   Beautiful redeeming grace.

VERSE 2:

Healer of the broken down,

G
   Of the orphans and oppressed,

A^7
   Find Him dining with the poor,

G
   Find Him here surrounding us.

CHORUS:

C F^2
   Hallelujah God is near.

C F^2
   Hallelujah God is near.

VERSE 3:

A^7
   From the ocean's depth to cedar trees,

G
   Fields of wheat along the plains,

A^7
   Praise to God from all the earth,

G
   Praise Him from the mountaintops.

(REPEAT CHORUS TWICE)

BRIDGE:

A^7 Am   F   Am   F

Am
   His radiance is greater

F
   Than anything on earth or sky.

Am
   Stars and moon will guard the night,

F
   Shining to the God on high.

Am
   Let true love break out in praise.

F
   Let it dance and praise His name.

Am
   All creation join to sing

F
   Hallelujah to the King.

(REPEAT CHORUS TWICE)

A^7 G^7

Hear Our Song

JADON LAVIK, STEVE HINDALONG and MARC BYRD

KEY OF (D)

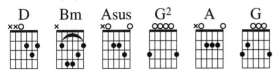

Sheet Music available at
WORSHIP TOGETHER.com

Scripture References

*Psalm 89:1-2
I will sing of the Lord's great love forever; with my mouth I will make your faithfulness known through all generations. I will declare that your love stands firm forever, that you established your faithfulness in heaven itself.*

VERSE 1:

D
In joyous surrender,

Bm
With our eyes fixed on You,

Asus
May our lives bring You glory,

G^2
To serve You in all that we do.

VERSE 2:

D
In joyous surrender,

Bm
With our hearts full of praise,

Asus
We sing of Your mercy,

G^2
We sing of Your love and Your grace.

CHORUS 1:

D   A
And Father, hear our song,

Bm G^2
A song of praise   to the Worthy One.

CONTINUED...

(REPEAT VERSE 1 & CHORUS 1)

CHORUS 2:

D   A
Father, we have come,

Bm G^2
To offer our lives to the Holy One.

BRIDGE:

(G   A   G   A) *1st time only*

           G   A
And we live   for Your glory,

           G   A
And we live   by Your love,

           G   A
And we sing   of Your glory,

           G   A
And we sing   of Your love.

(REPEAT CHORUS 1 & CHORUS 2)

(REPEAT BRIDGE)

Theme(s):
Commitment &
Dedication
Tempo:
112 bpm
Mid Up-Tempo
Played Key:
D
Vocal Range:

middle C

C# - F#

Similar Theme
Beauty For Ashes
The Servant King

Similar Tempo
Be Glorified
Song Of Love

Similar Key
Enter In
Rain Down

Scripture References

Psalms 146:7-10
[7]He upholds the cause of the oppressed and gives food to the hungry. The Lord sets prisoners free, [8]the Lord gives sight to the blind, the Lord lifts up those who are bowed down, the Lord loves the righteous. [9]The Lord watches over the alien and sustains the fatherless and the widow, but he frustrates the ways of the wicked. [10]The Lord reigns forever, your God, O Zion, for all generations. Praise the Lord.

Theme(s):
Adoration & Praise

Tempo:
102 bpm
Mid Up-Tempo

Played Key:
G

Vocal Range:
middle C

C - E

Similar Theme
Moment Of Glory
Sing To The King

Similar Tempo
Famous One
Overflow

Similar Key
Facedown
Wholly Yours

Hosanna (Praise Is Rising)
BRENTON BROWN and PAUL BALOCHE

KEY OF (G)

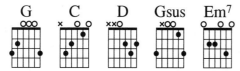

G   C   D   Gsus   Em[7]

VERSE 1:

G   C   G
Praise is rising, eyes are turning to You,   we turn to You.

                                               C   G
Hope is stirring, hearts are yearning for You,   we long for You.

PRE-CHORUS:

              D   C   G
'Cause when we see   You we find strength   to face the day,

              D   C   G   D
And in Your pres - ence all our fears   are washed away,   washed away.

CHORUS:

      Gsus   G   Em[7]   C
Ho - san - na, ho - sanna,

              G   D   Em[7]   C
You are the God   who saves us,   worthy of all   our praises.

      Gsus   G   Em[7]   C
Ho - san - na, ho - sanna,

              G   D   Em[7]   C
Come have Your way   among us.   We welcome You here   Lord Jesus.

VERSE 2:

G   C   G
Hear the sound of hearts returning to You,   we turn to You.

                                               C   G
In Your kingdom broken lives are made new,   you make all things new.

(REPEAT PRE-CHORUS & CHORUS)

How Can I Keep From Singing

CHRIS TOMLIN, MATT REDMAN and ED CASH

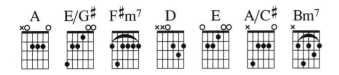

A   E/G#   F#m⁷   D   E   A/C#   Bm⁷

Capo 1 (A)

VERSE 1:

      A   E/G#
There is an endless song, echoes in my soul,

 F#m⁷   D
I hear the music ring.

      E   A   E/G#
And though the storms may come, I am holding on,

F#m⁷   E/G#   A   F#m⁷   D
To   the   rock   I   cling.

CHORUS:

A   E
How can I keep from singing Your   praise?

       D   A/C#
How can I ever say e - nough,

       D   E
how a - mazing is Your   love?

A   E
How can I keep from shouting Your   name?

       D   A/C#
I know I am loved by the King,

CHORUS TAG:

     D   E   A
And it makes my heart want to sing.

VERSE 2:

     A   E/G#
I will lift my eyes in the darkest night,

   F#m⁷   D
For I know my Savior lives.

    E   A
And I will walk with You

         E/G#
knowing You see me through,

   F#m⁷   E/G#   A   F#m⁷   D
And sing   the   songs   You   give.

(REPEAT CHORUS & CHORUS TAG)

CONTINUED...

BRIDGE:

       Bm⁷   A/C#   D   E
I can sing in the troubled times, sing when I win.

       Bm⁷   A/C#
I can   sing when I lose my step

      D   E
and I   fall down a - gain.

       Bm⁷   A/C#
I can   sing 'cause You pick me up,

D   E
sing 'cause You're there.

       Bm⁷   A/C#
I can   sing 'cause You hear me Lord,

       D   E
When I   call to You in pray - er.

       Bm⁷   A/C#
I can   sing with my last breath,

D   E   Bm⁷   A/C#
    Sing for I know that I'll   sing with the angels,

      D   E
And the saints around the throne.

(REPEAT CHORUS)

ENDING:

       D   E
And it makes my heart,

      D   A/C#
I am loved by the King,

      D   E
And it makes my heart,

      D   A/C#
I am loved by the King,

      D   E   A
And it makes my heart want to sing.

Yeah, I can sing.

Sheet Music available at
WORSHIP TOGETHER.com

Scripture References

Isaiah 12:5-6
⁵Sing to the Lord, for he has done glorious things; let this be known to all the world. ⁶Shout aloud and sing for joy, people of Zion, for great is the Holy One of Israel among you.

Psalm 30:11-12
¹¹You turned my wailing into dancing; you removed my sackcloth and clothed me with joy, ¹²that my heart may sing to You and not be silent. O Lord, my God, I will give You thanks forever.

Theme(s):
Adoration & Praise

Tempo:
dotted quarter 74 bpm
Mid Tempo

Played Key:
Bb

Vocal Range:

middle C

F - G

Similar Theme
Center
Give You Glory

Similar Tempo
Almighty God
Beautiful Lord

Similar Key
Almighty God
Everlasting God

Scripture References

Psalms 22:27-28
²⁷All the ends of the earth will remember and turn to the Lord, and all the families of the nations will bow down before him, ²⁸for dominion belongs to the Lord and he rules over the nations.

Isaiah 40:31
But those who hope in the Lord will renew their strength. They will saor on wings like eagles; they will run and not grow weary, they will walk and not be faint.

Theme(s):
Adoration & Praise
Tempo:
144 bpm
Up Tempo
Played Key:
A
Vocal Range:

middle C

C# - E

Similar Theme
Great God Of Wonders
Hosanna
(Praise Is Rising)

Similar Tempo
Closer
Declare Victory

Similar Key
Holy Moment
Marvelous Light

I Will Remember You

BRENTON BROWN

KEY OF (A)

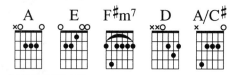

A   E   F#m⁷   D   A/C#

CHORUS 1:

```
              A            E
I will remem - ber You,
        F#m⁷                    D
always re  -  member You,
              A            E
I will remem - ber You,
                      F#m⁷       D
and all You've done      for me.
```

VERSE 1:

```
A       E     F#m⁷          D
 I will not  forget    all Your ben - efits,
A         E                   F#m⁷      D
 Even when  the storm surrounds     my soul.
A            E
 How You com - fort me,
F#m⁷        D
   heal all   my diseases,
A            E
 How You lift  me up
        F#m⁷              D
on ea  -  gle's wings.
```

(REPEAT CHORUS 1 TWICE)

VERSE 2:

```
A       E     F#m⁷          D
 I will not  forget    all Your ben - efits,
A            E                F#m⁷    D
 How You've cho - sen and adopt - ed me.
A            E
 Orphaned by  my sin,
F#m⁷              D
   Your grace has let   me in,
A            E
 And never once
        F#m⁷            D
have You aban - doned me.
```

CONTINUED...

(REPEAT CHORUS 1 TWICE)

BRIDGE:

```
A/C#              D              E
    I have tast - ed and I've seen
                F#m⁷
how You fa - ther faithfully,
A/C#                  D
    How You shep - herd those
        E            F#m⁷
who fear  Your name.
A/C#                  D              E
    When the shad - ow's start to fall
                F#m⁷
and my heart    begins to fail,
A/C#       D              E        F#m⁷
    I will lift  my eyes to You   again.
```

CHORUS 2:

```
                           A
And I will remem - ber You, always remember You,

I will remember You and all You've done for me.
                           A/C#
I will remember You,
        F#m⁷                    D
always re - member You,
                   A        A/C#
I will remem - ber You
                    F#m⁷        D
and all You've done    for me.
```

(REPEAT CHORUS 1 TWICE)

ENDING:

```
A    E   F#m⁷   D
Yeah.

A    E                 F#m⁷      D    A
          All You've done    for me,    yeah.
```

Jesus You Are Worthy

BRENTON BROWN

KEY OF (C)

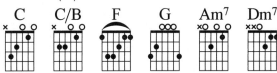

Sheet Music available at
WORSHIP TOGETHER.com

Scripture References

*Revelation 5:12
In a loud voice they
sang: "Worthy is the
Lamb, who was slain,
to receive power and
wealth and wisdom
and strength and
honor and glory and
praise!"*

VERSE:

         C   C/B
Jesus You are mercy. Jesus You are   justice.

         F   G   C
Jesus You are worthy. That is what You are.

You died alone to save me.

                           C/B
You rose so You could raise   me.

                     F
You did this all to make me

 G   C
A chosen child of God.

CHORUS:

                  F   G   C
(How)* Worthy is the Lamb that once was slain,   *last time only.*

            F   G   C
To receive all glory, pow'r, and praise.

                  F   G   Am⁷
For with Your blood You purchased us for God.

       (F   G   Am⁷)*   *last time only.*
(Jesus You are worthy. That is what You   are.)*

         F   G   C
Jesus You are worthy. That is what You are.

(REPEAT VERSE)

(REPEAT CHORUS)

BRIDGE:

        Dm⁷   Am⁷
Perfect sacri - fice crushed by God for us.

               F   G
Bearing in Your hurt all that I deserve.

           Dm⁷   Am⁷
Misjudged for my mis - deeds, You suffered silent - ly,

             F   G
The only guiltless man in all of history.

(REPEAT CHORUS)

Theme(s):
Resurrection &
Sacrifice
Tempo:
66 bpm
Slow Tempo
Played Key:
C
Vocal Range:

middle C

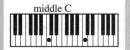

C - C

Similar Theme
Once Again
The Wonderful Cross

Similar Tempo
It Is Well
The Servant King

Similar Key
Much Of You
Wonderful Maker

Scripture References

Psalms 68:1
May God arise, may His enemies be scattered; may His foes flee before Him.

Psalms 68:20
Our God is a God who saves; from the Sovereign Lord comes escape from death.

Let God Arise

CHRIS TOMLIN, ED CASH and JESSE REEVES

KEY OF (A)

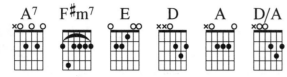

A⁷   F♯m⁷   E   D   A   D/A

Theme(s):
God's Attributes

Tempo:
144 bpm
Up Tempo

Played Key:
B

Vocal Range:

middle C

F# - F#

Similar Theme
Almighty God
Everything

Similar Tempo
Awesome Is The Lord
Most High

Similar Key
All Over The World
Blessed Be Your Name

Capo 2 (A)

VERSE 1:

$\quad\quad\quad\quad$ A⁷
Hear the ho - ly roar of God resound,

Watch the waters part before us now.

$\quad\quad\quad\quad\quad$ F♯m⁷
Come and see $\quad\quad$ what He has done for us,

$\quad\;$ E
Tell $\quad$ the world of His great love,

PRE-CHORUS:

$\quad\quad$ D $\quad\quad\quad$ F♯m⁷ $\quad\quad\quad$ E
Our God $\;$ is a God $\quad\quad$ who saves.

$\quad\quad$ D $\quad\quad\quad$ F♯m⁷ $\quad\quad\quad$ E
Our God $\;$ is a God $\quad\quad$ who saves.

CHORUS:

$\quad\quad\quad\quad$ A $\quad\quad\quad\quad$ D/A
Let God arise, $\quad$ Let God arise.

$\quad\quad\quad\quad\quad$ A⁷
Our God reigns $\quad$ now and forever,

$\quad\quad\quad$ D/A
He reigns $\quad\quad$ now and forever.

(G $\;$ A⁷ $\quad$ D $\quad\quad$ G $\;$ A⁷ $\quad$ D) $\quad$ *1st time only*

CONTINUED...

VERSE 2:

$\quad\quad\quad\quad$ A⁷
His en - emies will run for sure,

The church will stand, She will endure.

$\quad\quad\quad\quad\quad$ F♯m⁷
He holds $\quad\quad$ the keys of life, our Lord,

$\quad\quad\quad\quad$ E
Death has $\;$ no sting, no final word,

(REPEAT PRE-CHORUS)

(REPEAT CHORUS TWICE)

INSTRUMENTAL:

D $\;$ F♯m⁷ $\;$ E $\quad\quad\quad$ D $\;$ F♯m⁷ $\;$ E

(REPEAT PRE-CHORUS TWICE)

(REPEAT CHORUS TWICE)

ENDING:

G $\quad$ A⁷ $\quad\quad$ D $\quad\quad\quad$ G $\quad$ A⁷ $\quad\quad$ D

G $\quad$ A⁷ $\quad\quad$ D $\quad\quad\quad$ G $\quad$ A⁷ $\quad\quad$ D

A

Made To Worship

CHRIS TOMLIN, STEPHAN SHARP and ED CASH

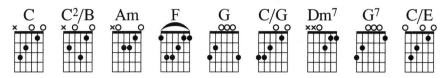

C   C²/B   Am   F   G   C/G   Dm⁷   G⁷   C/E

VERSE 1:

    C   C²/B
Be - fore the day, be - fore the light,
   Am   F   G
Be - fore the world revolved around the sun.
C   C²/B
God on high stepped down in - to time,
                 Am
And wrote the sto - ry
                       F   G
of His love for everyone.

PRE-CHORUS:

F   G
   He has filled our hearts with wonder,
F   C/G   F
   so that we al - ways re - member:

CHORUS:

C
You and I were made to worship,
F
You and I are called to love,
Dm⁷   G⁷
You and I are forgiven and free.
   C
When you and I embrace surrender,
   F
When you and I choose to believe,
   Dm⁷   G⁷
Then you and I will see

(you and I will see) *3rd time only*

who we were meant to be.

VERSE 2:

C   C²/B
  All we are and all we have,
  Am   F
Is all a gift from God that we receive.
C   C²/B
Brought to life we open up   our eyes,
          Am   F   G
To see the maj - esty and glory of the King.

CONTINUED...

(REPEAT PRE-CHORUS)

(REPEAT CHORUS)

BRIDGE:

Dm⁷
   Even the rocks cry out,
C/E
   even the heavens shout,
F   G⁷
   At the sound of His Holy name.
Dm⁷
   So let every voice sing out,
C/E
   let every knee bow down,
F   G⁷
   He is worthy of all our praise.

(REPEAT CHORUS TWICE)

ENDING:

           F   Dm⁷   G⁷
Yeah,   we were meant to be,   oo.
           C   F
You and I,   you and I,
        Dm⁷   G⁷
yeah,   yeah, oo.
                      C
We were meant to be.

Sheet Music available at

Scripture References

John 4:23-24
[23]*Yet a time is coming and has now come when the true worshipers will worship the Father in spirit and truth, for they are the kind of worshipers the Father seeks.* [24]*God is spirit, and his worshipers must worship in spirit and in truth.*

Theme(s):
Faith & Trust

Tempo:
86 bpm
Mid Tempo

Played Key:
C

Vocal Range:

middle C
E - G

Similar Theme
It Is Well
Worth It All

Similar Tempo
God Of Justice
Holy Moment

Similar Key
Beautiful Lord
Jesus You Are Worthy

Sheet Music available at
WORSHIP TOGETHER.com

Scripture References

*Romans 5:1-2
Therefore, since we
have been justified
through faith, we
have peace with God
through our Lord Jesus
Christ, through whom
we have gained access
by faith into this grace
in which we now stand.
And we rejoice in the
hope of the glory of
God.*

*1 John 3:3
Everyone who has
this hope in him
purifies himself, just as
he is pure.*

Theme(s):
Grace & Mercy

Tempo:
55 bpm
Slow Tempo

Played Key:
D

Vocal Range:

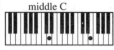

D - E

Similar Theme
Beautiful Lord
Make Me Like You

Similar Tempo
Communion
Jesus You Are Worthy

Similar Key
Carried To The Table
Hear Our Song

Outrageous Grace

GODFREY BIRTILL

KEY OF (D)

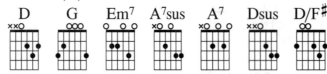

D   G   Em⁷   A⁷sus   A⁷   Dsus   D/F♯

VERSE 1:

     D   G   D
There's a lot of pain, but a lot more heal - ing,
     Em⁷   A⁷sus
There's a lot of trouble,
    A⁷   D   A⁷sus   A⁷
but a lot more peace.
     D   G   D
There's a lot of hate, but a lot more lov - ing,
     Em⁷   A⁷sus
There's a lot of sin,
    A⁷   Dsus   D
but a lot more grace.

CHORUS:

     A⁷sus   D
Oh, out - rageous grace!
     A⁷sus   D
Oh, out - rageous grace!
      G   D/F♯ Em⁷   D/F♯   A⁷sus A⁷
Love un - furled by   heav - en's   hand.
     A⁷sus   D
Oh, out - rageous grace!
     A⁷sus   D
Oh, out - rageous grace!
      G   D/F♯ Em⁷   D/F♯   A⁷sus
Through my Je - sus   I   can   stand.
(A⁷)*

      1st & 2nd times only

VERSE 2:

     D   G   D
There's a lot of fear, but a lot more free - dom,
     Em⁷   A⁷sus
There's a lot of darkness,
    A⁷   D   A⁷sus   A⁷
but a lot more light.
     D   G D
There's a lot of cloud, but a lot more vi - sion,
     Em⁷   A⁷sus
There's a lot of perishing,
    A⁷   Dsus   D
but a lot more life.

CONTINUED...

(REPEAT CHORUS)

BRIDGE:

                   D
There's an enemy,
                        G   D
That seeks to kill   what it can't con - trol.
    Em⁷   A⁷sus
It twists and turns
         A⁷   G   D
Making mountains out of mole - hills.

But I will call on the Lord,
       G   D
Who is worthy of praise;
  Em⁷   A⁷sus   A⁷   Dsus D
I run to Him   and I am saved.

(REPEAT CHORUS)

D

Ready For You

JON MICAH SUMRALL

Sheet Music available at
WORSHIP TOGETHER.com

KEY OF (C)

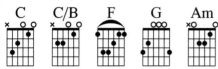

C   C/B   F   G   Am

Scripture References

Psalms 51:10
Create in me
a pure heart, O God,
and renew a steadfast
spirit within me.

CONTINUED...

(REPEAT PRE-CHORUS & CHORUS)

VERSE 1:

C   C/B   F   G
Lord, You take my heart away   with Your   love.
    C   C/B   F   G
And I am willing to put all my faith in Your   plan.

PRE-CHORUS:

Am   G   F
  Come and take   my life.
Am   G   F   G
  Make my soul   refreshed in truth   now.

CHORUS:

C   G   F
  I am rea - dy for You.
C   G   F   G
  Take my heart   and make me new   now.
C   G   F
  I am rea - dy for You
      Am   G   F
To come   and fill my soul.
(C   C/B   F   G) *1st time only*

VERSE 2:

C   C/B   F   G
Cleanse all of my mind that is not   of   You.
C   C/B
Break me, teaching me how to find rest
F   G
  In Your   hands.

BRIDGE:

         Am   G   F   G
Won't You come and fill my soul.
Am   C
    Whatever it takes
               F   G
I'm needing to make   Your will be done.
              Am   C
And I'm letting go   of my control
        F   G
For I see   what You've done in me.

(REPEAT CHORUS)

ENDING:

C   G   F
  I am rea - dy for You. (I am ready for You.)
C   G   F   G
  Take my heart   and make me new   now.
C   G   F
  I am rea - dy for You. (I am ready for You.)
      Am   G   F
To come   and fill my soul.
 Am   G   F
(Come and fill my soul.)
         Am   G   F   G   C
Won't you come and fill my soul.

Theme(s):
Prayer & Renewal

Tempo:
80 bpm
Mid Tempo

Played Key:
C

Vocal Range:

middle C

C - G

Similar Theme
Be Lifted High
Closer

Similar Tempo
Give Me Jesus
Made To Worship

Similar Key
Give Me Jesus
Jesus You Are Worthy

Scripture References

1 Peter 1:3-5
³Praise be to the God and Father of our Lord Jesus Christ! In his great mercy he has given us new birth into a living hope through the resurrection of Jesus Christ from the dead, ⁴and into an inheritance that can never perish, spoil or fade-kept in heaven for you, ⁵who through faith are shielded by God's power until the coming of the salvation that is ready to be revealed in the last time.

Theme(s):
Resurrection & Sacrifice
Tempo:
126 bpm
Up Tempo
Played Key:
G
Vocal Range:
middle C

D - E

Similar Theme
Jesus You Are Worthy
Once Again

Similar Tempo
All We Need
Give You Glory

Similar Key
Maker Of All Things
We Want To See Jesus
Lifted High

Resurrection Day
MATT MAHER

KEY OF (G)

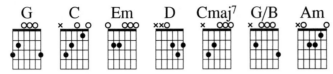

G   C   Em   D   Cmaj⁷   G/B   Am

VERSE 1:

G
  It's the weight of Your glory,

Brings the proud to their knees,

And the light of revelation,

Lets the blind man see.

C
  It's the power of the cross,

Breaks away death's embrace,

And we celebrate our freedom,

Dancing on an empty grave.

PRE-CHORUS:

Em   D
Roll away the stone,

Cmaj⁷   D
Roll away the stone.

CHORUS:

    G   G/B   C   D
We sing for joy,   we shout Your name,

    G   G/B   Em   D
We cele - brate Your resurrection   day.

    G   G/B   C   D
We sing for joy,   we shout Your name,

    G   G/B   C   D   G
We cele - brate Your resur - rection   day.

GUITAR SOLO:

G   C   G   C   G   C   G   C

CONTINUED...

VERSE 2:

G
  You declare what is holy,

You declare what is good,

In the sight of all the nations,

You declare that You are God.

C
  It's the power in Your Blood,

Breaks away sin's embrace,

And we celebrate our freedom,

Dancing on our broken chains.

(REPEAT PRE-CHORUS & CHORUS)

Em   D   Am   Em   D   Am

(REPEAT CHORUS TWICE)

(REPEAT GUITAR SOLO)

G

Resurrection Hymn (See, What a Morning)

STUART TOWNEND and KEITH GETTY

Sheet Music available at
WORSHIP **TOGETHER** .com

Scripture References

Matthew 28:6
He is not here;
he has risen, just as
he said. Come and see
the place where he lay.

KEY OF (D)

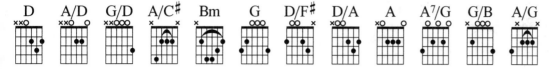

D   A/D   G/D   A/C#   Bm   G   D/F#   D/A   A   A7/G   G/B   A/G

CONTINUED...

VERSE 1:

D   A/D   G/D   D
See, what the morning, gloriously bright,

A/C#   Bm   G   D/F#   G   D/A   A
With the dawn - ing of hope   in Je - rusa - lem;

D   A/D   G/D   D
Folded the graveclothes, tomb filled with light,

A/C#   Bm   G   D/F#
As the an - gels an - nounce

G   D/A   A   A7/G
Christ is ris - en!

D/F#   A/G   G   D/F#
  See God's sal - va - tion plan,

G   D/F#
wrought in love,

G   D/F#   G   D/A   A   A/G
Borne in pain,   paid in sacri - fice,

D/F#   A/G   G D/F# G D/F#
  Fulfilled in Christ,   the Man,   for He lives:

G   D/A   A   D
Christ is risen   from the dead!

A/D   G/D   G   A

VERSE 2:

D   A/D   G/D   D
See Mary weeping, "Where is He laid?"

A/C#   Bm   G   D/F#   G   D/A   A
As in sor - row she turns   from the empty tomb;

D   A/D   G/D   D
Hears a voice speaking, calling her name;

A/C#   Bm   G
It's the Mas - ter,

D/F#   G   D/A   A   A7/G
  the Lord   raised to life a - gain!

D/F#   A/G   G   D/F#
  The voice that spans   the years,

G   D/F#
speaking life,

G   D/F#   G   D/A   A   A/G
Stirring hope,   bringing peace to us,

D/F#   A/G   G   D/F#
  Will sound 'til He   ap - pears,

G   D/F#
for He lives,

G   D/A   A   D
Christ is risen   from the dead!

A/D   G/D   G   A

VERSE 3:

D   A/D   G/D   D
One with the Father,   Ancient of Days,

A/C#   Bm   G
Through the Spir - it

D/F#   G   D/A   A
who clothes   faith with certain - ty,

D   A/D   G/D   D
Honor and blessing, glory and praise

A/C#   Bm   G
To the King   crowned

D/F#   G   D/A   A   A7/G
with power   and au - thori - ty.

D/F#   A/G   G   D/F#
  And we are raised   with Him,

G   D/F#
death is dead,

G   D/F#   G   D/A   A   A/G
Love was won,   Christ has con - quered.

D/F#   A/G   G   D/F#
  And we shall reign   with Him,

G   D/F#
for He lives,

G   D/A   A   D
Christ is risen   from the dead!

A/D   D

Theme(s):
Resurrection
& Sacrifice
Tempo:
dotted quarter 94 bpm
Mid Tempo
Played Key:
D
Vocal Range:

middle C

A - D

Similar Theme
Mighty Is The Power
Of The Cross
My Drink

Similar Tempo
Beautiful Lord
God Of Justice

Similar Key
Carried To The Table
Outrageous Grace

Scripture References

John 15:13
Greater love has no one than this, that he lay down his life for his friends.

See His Love

TOM LOCKLEY

KEY OF (Bm)

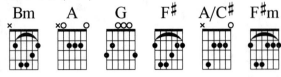

Bm A G F# A/C# F#m

VERSE 1:

Bm   A
See His love nailed to a cross,
            G
Perfect and blameless life
      A
Given as sacrifice.
Bm   A
See Him there all in the name of Love,
            G
Broken, yet glorious,
      A
All for the sake of us.

CHORUS:

Bm   G
This is Jesus in His glory,
A   F#
King of heaven, dying for me.
Bm   G
It is finished, He has done it.
A   F#   Bm
Death is beaten, heaven beckons me.

VERSE 2:

Bm   A
Greater love no one could ever show.
           G
Mercy so undeserved,
      A
Freedom I should not know.
Bm   A
All my sin, all of my hidden shame
          G
Died with Him on the cross.
      A
Eternity won for us.

(REPEAT CHORUS)

CHANNEL:

Bm   A/C#
   Such love,   such love,
F#m   G
   Such love is this for me.

(REPEAT CHANNEL 3 TIMES)

(REPEAT CHORUS)

Theme(s):
Resurrection &
Sacrifice
Tempo:
144 bpm
Up Tempo
Played Key:
Bm
Vocal Range:

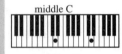

middle C

D - D

Similar Theme
Mighty Is The Power Of The Cross
Resurrection Day

Similar Tempo
Let God Arise
Resurrection Day

Similar Key
Give You Glory
The Wonderful Cross

Shine

MATT REDMAN

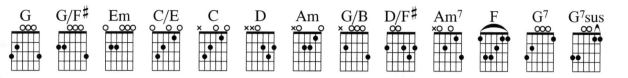

Sheet Music available at WORSHIP TOGETHER.com

Capo 1 (G)

VERSE:

G   G/F#
Lord we have seen the rising sun,

  Em   C/E Em
Awakening the early dawn,

 C   G D
And we're rising up to give You praise.

     G   G/F#
Lord we have seen the stars and moon,

     Em   C/E Em
See how they shine, they shine for You.

    C   G D
And You're calling us to do the same,

PRE-CHORUS:

    Am
So we rise up with a song,

   G/B
And we rise up with a cry,

    C
And we're giv - ing You our lives.

CHORUS 1:

     G
We will shine like stars in the universe,

     D/F#
Holding out   Your truth in the darkest place.

   Am7
We'll be living for Your glory,

      C
Jesus we'll be living for Your glory.

(REPEAT VERSE, PRE-CHORUS & CHORUS 1)

CHORUS 2

     G
We will burn so bright with Your praise, oh, God,

     D/F#
And declare   Your light to this broken world.

    F
We'll be living for Your glory,

     C
Jesus, we'll be living for Your glory.

CONTINUED...

BRIDGE:

      Am
Like the sun so radiantly,

       G/B
Sending light for all to see,

      C
Let Your Ho - ly Church arise.

   Am
Ex - ploding into life,

       G/B
Like a su - pernova's light,

      C
Set Your Ho - ly Church on fire,

(REPEAT BRIDGE)

       G
We will shine.

       G7
We will shine.

(REPEAT CHORUS 1, CHORUS 2 & PRE-CHORUS)

        G
Jesus, we will shine.

Scripture References

Philippians 2:15
So that you may become blameless and pure, children of God without fault in a crooked and depraved generation, in which you shine like stars in the universe.

Matthew 5:16
In the same way, let your light shine before men, that they may see your good deeds and praise your Father in heaven.

Theme(s):
Church & Unity

Tempo:
80 bpm
Mid Tempo

Played Key:
Ab

Vocal Range:

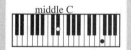

Eb - F

Similar Theme
All Over The World
We Will Worship Him

Similar Tempo
Everything Glorious
How Can I Keep From Singing

Similar Key
Declare Victory
I Will Never Be The Same

Scripture References

John 1:4
In him was life,
and that life
was the light of men.

John 6:69
We believe and
know that you are
the Holy One of God."

Son Of God

TIM NEUFELD, JON NEUFELD, ED CASH and GORDON COCHRAN

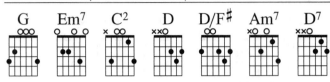

G   Em⁷   C²   D   D/F#   Am⁷   D⁷

Capo 1 (G)

Theme(s):
Adoration & Praise

Tempo:
84 bpm
Mid Tempo

Played Key:
Ab

Vocal Range:

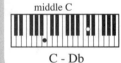

middle C

C - Db

Similar Theme
Sing a Song
Our Love is Loud

Similar Tempo
Beautiful Lord
Made To Worship

Similar Key
Declare Victory
Shine

VERSE 1:

G
  Son of God, shaper of the stars,

Em⁷
     You alone, the dweller of my heart.

C²
    Mighty king, how beautiful You are,

D   C²
  How beautiful.

VERSE 2:

G
  Son of God, the Father's gift to us,

Em⁷
     You alone were broken on the altar of love.

C²
    Precious lamb, our freedom's in Your blood,

D C²   D
  It's   in Your blood.

CHORUS:

G   C²
Jesus, Oh holy one,

 D   G   D/F#
I sing to You, for - given.

Em⁷   Am⁷
Savior, I'm overcome

    C²   D⁷   (G)*
With Your great love for me.   **1st & 3rd times*

VERSE 3:

G
  Son of God, strength beyond compare,

Em⁷
     You alone the darkness cannot bear.

C²
    Lord of all, Your kindness draws me near,

D C²
  It draws me.

(CONTINUED...)

VERSE 4:

G
  Son of God, prophecy of old,

Em⁷
     You alone, redeemer of my soul.

C²
    Come again and lead Your people home,

D   C²   D
  Come   lead us home.

(REPEAT CHORUS)

BRIDGE:

          G   D/F#
You are worthy, You are worthy,

         Em⁷   C²
You are worthy of all my praise.

          G   D/F#
You are beautiful, You are beautiful,

         Em⁷   C²
I will lift up my hands and sing.

(REPEAT BRIDGE)

(REPEAT CHORUS)

ENDING:

With Your great love,

With Your great love,

With Your great love.

Sound Of Melodies

LEELAND MOORING, JACK MOORING and STEVE WILSON

Sheet Music available at WORSHIP TOGETHER.com

KEY OF (D)

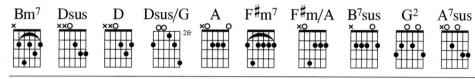

Bm⁷   Dsus   D   Dsus/G   A   F#m⁷   F#m/A   B⁷sus   G²   A⁷sus

Scripture References

Isaiah 24:16
From the ends of the earth we hear singing "Glory to the Righteous One."

Psalms 19:1
The heavens declare the glory of God; the skies proclaim the work of his hands.

CONTINUED...

VERSE 1:

Bm⁷   Dsus   D
We who were called to be Your   people,

Bm⁷   Dsus   D
Struggling sinners and thieves.

   Bm⁷   Dsus   D
We're lifted   up from the ashes,

   Bm⁷   Dsus   D
And out came the song of the re - deemed,

Bm⁷   Dsus/G   D
   The song of the redeemed.

Bm⁷   Dsus/G

CHORUS:

              D
Can you hear the sound of melodies,

    A   F#m⁷
Oh, the sound of melodies rising up to You,

    F#m/A   B⁷sus   G²
Rising up   to   You,   God?

    D
The sound of melodies,

    A   F#m⁷
Oh, the sound of melodies rising up to You,

    F#m/A   B⁷sus   G²   D
Rising up   to   You,   God?

VERSE 2:

   Bm⁷   Dsus/G   D
Oh, we have caught a reve - lation,

    Bm⁷   Dsus/G   D
That nothing can separate us from.

    Bm⁷   Dsus/G   D
The love we re - ceived through sal - vation,

   Bm⁷   Dsus/G   D
It fills your daughters and Your sons,

Bm⁷   Dsus/G   D
   Your daughters and Your   sons.

Bm⁷   Dsus/G

(REPEAT CHORUS)

BRIDGE:

                                           A
The sound of Your love, the sound of Your love,

                   Bm⁷   G²
Is what You're   hear - ing.

D   A
   The sound of Your sons, the sound of Your sons,

                   Bm⁷   G²
You've won Your   chil - dren.

D   A
   The sound of Your love, the sound of Your love,

                   Bm⁷   G²
Is what You're   hear - ing.

D   A
   Your daughters in love, Your daughters in love,

                   Bm⁷   G²
You've won Your   chil - dren.

CHANNEL:

         D
The sound of melodies,

         A⁷sus   A   F#m⁷
Oh, the sound of melo - dies rising up to You.

    A   Bm⁷   G²   D
Rising up to You,   God,

A   F#m⁷   A   Bm⁷   G²
   Rising up to You,   God.

REFRAIN:

    D   A
La, la, la, la, la, la, la, la, la, la, la, la.

         F#m⁷   F#m/A   B⁷sus   G²
La, la, la, la, la, la, la, la, la,   la,   la,   la.

(REPEAT REFRAIN)

D

Theme(s):
Adoration & Praise

Tempo:
dotted quarter 82 bpm
Mid Tempo

Played Key:
D

Vocal Range:

middle C

C - B

Similar Theme
Adoration
Hosanna
(Praise Is Rising)

Similar Tempo
Ready For You
Shine

Similar Key
Hear Our Song
Resurrection Hymn

Scripture References

Psalms 139:23
Search me, O God, and know my heart; test me and know my anxious thoughts.

Romans 12:2
Do not conform any longer to the pattern of this world, but be transformed by the renewing of your mind, then you will be able to test and approve what God's will is - his good, pleasing and perfect will.

Theme(s):
Prayer & Renewal

Tempo:
68 bpm
Slow Mid-Tempo

Played Key:
C

Vocal Range:

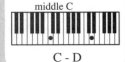
middle C

C - D

Similar Theme
Be Lifted High
Closer

Similar Tempo
Like The Angels
Pour My Love On You

Similar Key
Give Me Jesus
Made To Worship

Speak, O Lord
KEITH GETTY and STUART TOWNEND

KEY OF (C)

F/A   G/B   C² · F · C · Am · C/E · G · G/F · Gsus/F · G⁹/F · C²/E · Gsus · F²

CONTINUED...

VERSE 1:

F/A G/B C²   F   C
Speak, O   Lord, as we come to You,
         F   C   Am   G/B
To re - ceive the food   of Your holy word.
F/A G/B C²   F   C
Take Your truth, plant it deep in us;
         F   C/E F   G   C
Shape and fashion us   in Your like-ness,
C/E   G   G/F C/E
That the light of   Christ
         Gsus/F   G⁹/F   C²/E
might be seen   to-day,
      G   G/F C/E   Am   Gsus G
In our acts of   love and our deeds of faith.
F/A G/B C²   F   C
Speak, O   Lord, and ful-fill in us
         F   C/E
all your purposes,
F   Gsus   G C
For Your glo -   ry.
F²

C²/E   F²   Gsus   G

VERSE 2:

F/A G/B C²   F   C
Teach us   Lord full o-bedience,
         F   C   Am   G/B
Holy rev-erence,   true hu-mility.
F/A G/B C²   F   C
Test our   thoughts and our attitudes,
         F   C/E F   G   C
In the radiance   of Your puri - ty.
C/E   G   G/F C/E
Cause our faith to   rise,
         Gsus/F   G⁹/F   C²/E
Cause our eyes   to see,
      G   G/F C/E   Am   Gsus G
Your ma-jes-tic   love and au-thor - i - ty.
F/A G/B C²   F   C
Words of   power that can never fail;
         F   C/E F Gsus   G C
Let their truth pre-vail   over un -   belief.
F²

C²/E   F²   Gsus   G

VERSE 3:

F/A G/B C²   F   C
Speak, O   Lord, and re-new our minds;
         F   C
Help us grasp the heights
              Am   G/B
of Your plans for us.
F/A G/B C²   F   C
Truths un - changed from the dawn of time,
         F   C/E F   G   C
That will echo down   through e-terni-ty.
C/E   G   G/F C/E
And by grace we'll stand
              Gsus/F   G⁹/F   C²/E
on Your prom   -   is-es;
      G   G/F C/E   Am   Gsus G
And by faith we'll   walk as You walk with us.
F/A G/B C²   F   C
Speak, O   Lord, till Your church is built,
         F   C/E F   Gsus   G C
And the earth is filled   with Your glo -   ry.
F²

C²/E   F²   Gsus   G

C

Strong Tower

MARC BYRD, MARK LEE, JON MICAH SUMRALL and AARON SPRINKLE

KEY OF (E)

B   A   C#m⁷   F#m⁷   E/G#   A²   E   Bsus

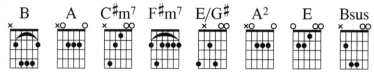

Scripture References

Psalms 31:2-3
Turn your ear to me, come quickly to my rescue; be my rock of refuge, a strong fortress to save me. Since you are my rock and my fortress, for the sake of your name lead and guide me.

Proverbs 18:10
The name of the Lord is a strong tower; the righteous run to it and are safe.

VERSE 1:

B   A   C#m⁷
When I wan - der through the des - ert
              B
And I'm longing for my home,
         A   C#m⁷
All my dreams have gone a - stray,
B   A   C#m⁷
When I'm strand - ed in the val - ley
            B
And I'm tired and all alone,
       A   C#m⁷
It seems like I've lost my way,
F#m⁷   E/G#   A²
   I go running to   Your moun - tain,
F#m⁷   E/G#   A
   Where Your mercy sets   me free.

CHORUS:

             E
You are my strong tow - er,
          C#m⁷
A shelter over me,
          A²
Beautiful and might - y, everlasting King.
      Bsus   E
You are my   strong tow - er,
            C#m⁷
A fortress when I'm weak.
           A
Your name is true and ho - ly,
      B   C#m⁷   A
And Your face is all   I   see.

VERSE 2:

B   A   C#m⁷
  In the mid - dle of my dark - ness,
               B
In the midst of all my fear,
          A   C#m⁷
You're my ref - uge and my   hope.
B   A   C#m⁷
  When the storm of life is rag - ing
              B
And the thunder's all I hear,
        A   C#m⁷
You speak softly   to my   soul.
F#m⁷   E/G#   A²
   Now I'm running to   Your moun - tain
F#m⁷   E/G#   A
   Where Your mercy sets   me free.

CONTINUED...

(REPEAT CHORUS)

        B   C#m⁷   A
And Your face is all   I   see.
          B   C#m⁷ A²
Yeah, Your face is all   I   see.
F#m⁷   E/G#   A
   I go running to   Your moun - tain,
F#m⁷   E/G#   A²
   Where Your mercy sets   me free.

(REPEAT CHORUS)

B   C#m⁷   A

Theme(s):
Faith & Trust

Tempo:
76 bpm
Slow Mid-Tempo

Played Key:
E

Vocal Range:

middle C

B - B

Similar Theme
I Believe In You
Holy Moment

Similar Tempo
As We Seek Your Face
Speak O Lord

Similar Key
Center
Great God Of Wonders

Scripture References

Luke 15:20
So he got up and went to his father. "But while he was still a long way off, his father saw him and was filled with compassion for him; he ran to his son, threw his arms around him and kissed him."

1 Samuel 2:8
He raises the poor from the dust and lifts the needy from the ash heap; he seats them with princes and has them inherit a throne of honor. "For the foundation of the earth are the Lord's; upon them he has set the world.

Theme(s):
Suffering & Trials

Tempo:
92 bpm
Mid Tempo

Played Key:
B

Vocal Range:

middle C
C# - B

Similar Theme
Like The Angels
When The Tears Fall

Similar Tempo
Almighty God
God Of Justice

Similar Key
All Over The World
Let God Arise

Tears Of The Saints

LEELAND MOORING and JACK MOORING

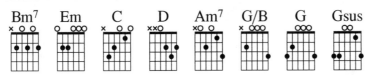

Bm⁷   Em   C   D   Am⁷   G/B   G   Gsus

Capo 4 (G)

VERSE 1:

Bm⁷   Em
    There are many prodigal sons,

        C
On our city streets they run,

            D
Searching for shel - ter.

          Em
There are homes broken down,

        C
People's hopes have fallen to the ground,

    D   Am⁷
From fail - ures. This is an e - mergency!

CHORUS:

G/B   C
    There are tears from the saints,

      G   D
For the lost and unsaved,

                Am⁷
We're crying for them come back home,

              C   D
We're crying for them come back home,

            C
And all Your children will stretch out their hands,

          G
And pick up   the crippled man,

            Am⁷
Father we will lead them home,

          C   D   Bm⁷
Father we will lead them home,

INTERLUDE 1:

Em   C   D

(CONTINUED...)

VERSE 2:

Bm⁷   Em
    There are schools full of hatred,

        C   D
Even churches have forsaken love and mer - cy.

              Em
May we see this generation,

        C
In its state of desperation.

              D   Am⁷
For Your glo - ry. This is an e - mergency!

(REPEAT CHORUS)

INTERLUDE 2:

Em   D   Gsus   G

BRIDGE:

D   Gsus   G
Sinners, reach out   your hands!

D   Gsus   G
Children in Christ   you stand!

D   Gsus   G
Sinners, reach out   your hands!

D   Em   C   Am
Children in Christ   you stand!

(REPEAT CHORUS)

ENDING:

C
    And all Your children will stretch out their hands,

              G   D
And pick up   the crippled man,

                Am⁷
Father we will lead them home,

                C
Father we will lead them home,

D   Bm⁷   C

Unashamed

TIM NEUFELD and DOUG MCKELVEY

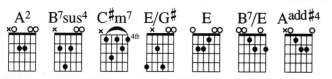

A²   B⁷sus⁴   C#m⁷   E/G#   E   B⁷/E   Aadd#4

Scripture References

Hebrews 10:19-22 Therefore, brothers, since we have confidence to enter the Most Holy Place by the blood of Jesus, by a new and living way opened for us through the curtain, that is, his body, and since we have a great priest over the house of God, let us draw near to God with a sincere heart in full assurance of faith, having our hearts sprinkled to cleanse us from a guilty conscience and having ouir bodies washed with pure water.

Capo 1 (E)

VERSE 1:

A²   B⁷sus   C#m⁷   E/G#
I have not much to offer You.

A²   B⁷sus   C#m⁷ E/G#
Not near what You deserve,

A²   B⁷sus   C#m⁷   E/G#
But still I come be - cause Your cross

A²   B⁷sus   E
has placed in me my worth.

VERSE 2:

A²   B⁷sus   C#m⁷   E/G#
O Christ, my king of sympathy

A²   B⁷sus   C#m⁷ E/G#
whose wounds se - cure my peace,

A²   B⁷sus   C#m⁷   E/G#
Your grace ex - tends to call me friend,

A²   B⁷sus   E
Your mercy sets me free.

CHORUS:

A²   B⁷sus
And I know   I'm weak,

C#m⁷
I know I'm unworthy

E/G#   A²   B⁷sus   C#m⁷
to call   u - pon Your name.

E/G#   A²   B⁷sus
But because   of grace,

C#m⁷
be - cause of Your mercy,

E/G#   A²   B⁷sus   E
I stand   here un - ashamed.

INTERLUDE:

A²   B⁷sus   C#m⁷

A²   B⁷sus   C#m⁷

(CONTINUED...)

VERSE 3:

A²   B⁷sus   C#m⁷   E/G#
I can't ex - plain this kind of love,

A²   B⁷sus   C#m⁷ E/G#
I'm humbled and amazed

B⁷sus   C#m⁷   E/G#
that You'd come down from heaven's heights

A²   B⁷sus   E
and greet me face to face.

(REPEAT CHORUS TWICE)

BRIDGE:

B⁷/E   E   B⁷/E

E   A²   E   A²

REFRAIN:

E   A²
Here I am,   at Your feet,

E   A²
in my bro - kenness complete.

(REPEAT REFRAIN SEVEN TIMES)

ENDING:

Aadd#4
At Your feet, I'm complete.

Theme(s):
Grace & Mercy

Tempo:
half note 80 bpm
Slow Mid-Tempo

Played Key:
F

Vocal Range:

middle C

E - C

Similar Theme
Beautiful Lord
Outrageous Grace

Similar Tempo
As We Seek Your Face
Strong Tower

Similar Key
As We Seek Your Face
God Of Justice

Scripture References

Psalms 86:8
Among the gods there is none like you, O Lord; no deeds can compare with yours.

Colossians 1:16
For by him all things were created; things in heaven and on earth, visible and invisible, whether thrones or powers or rulers or authorities; all things by him and for him.

Theme(s):
Adoration & Praise

Tempo:
70 bpm
Slow Mid-Tempo

Played Key:
Eb

Vocal Range:

middle C

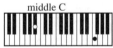

Bb - F

Similar Theme
Adoration
Sound Of Melodies

Similar Tempo
As We Seek Your Face
Give You Glory

Similar Key
Beauty For Ashes
Come And Listen

Uncreated One
CHRIS TOMLIN and J.D. WALT

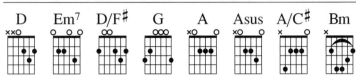

D   Em⁷   D/F♯   G   A   Asus   A/C♯   Bm

Capo 1 (D)

VERSE 1:

D Em⁷ D/F♯ G A D
Ho - ly   Uncre - at - ed One,

    G   D/F♯   Asus A
Your beauty fills   the skies.

      D   A/C♯ Bm   Asus
But the glory of   Your majes - ty

    G   Asus A   D
Is the mercy in   Your eyes.

VERSE 2:

    D Em⁷ D/F♯ G A D
And wor - thy   Uncre - at - ed One,

    G   D/F♯   Asus A
From heaven to earth come down.

    D   A/C♯ Bm   Asus
You laid a - side Your royal - ty

    G   Asus A   D
To wear the sin - ner's crown.

CHORUS 1:

    A   G   D
And O Great God be glori - fied,

    A   G A   D
Our lives laid down, Your's magnified.

    A   G A Bm
And O Great God be lift - ed   high,

G   Asus A   D
There is none like You.

(D   Bm Asus A   D   Bm Asus A)
(1st time only)

VERSE 3:

D Em⁷ D/F♯ G A   D
Je - sus,   Savior, God's own son,

G   D/F♯   Asus A
Risen, reign - ing Lord.

    D   A/C♯ Bm   Asus
Sus-tainer of the Universe

      G   Asus   A   D
By the power of   Your word.

CONTINUED...

(REPEAT CHORUS 1)

CHANNEL:

D   Bm   Asus A   D   Bm

Asus   A   D   Bm
There is none like You,

Asus   A   D   Bm Asus A
There is none like You,

VERSE 4:

    D Em⁷ D/F♯ G   A   D
And when we   see Your match - less face,

    G   D/F♯   Asus   A
In speechless awe   we'll   stand.

    D   A/C♯ Bm   Asus
And there we'll bow with grateful   hearts,

    G   Asus A D
Un - to the Great I Am.

CHORUS 2:

    A   G   D
And O Great God be glori - fied,

    A   G A   D
Our lives laid down, Your's magnified.

    A   G A Bm
And O Great God be lift - ed   high,

G   Asus A Bm
There is none like You.

G   Asus A   D
There is none like You.

ENDING:

Bm Asus A   D

Bm   Asus   A   D
        There is none like You,

Bm Asus A   D   Bm Asus A   D

Unwavering
MATT MAHER

Sheet Music available at
WORSHIP TOGETHER.com

KEY OF (E)

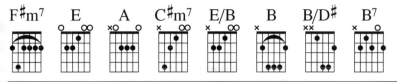

F♯m⁷ E A C♯m⁷ E/B B B/D♯ B⁷

Scripture References

Matthew 5:3
Blessed are the poor in spirit, for theirs is the kingdom of heaven.

Matthew 5:5
Blessed are the meek, for they will inherit the earth.

CONTINUED...

VERSE 1:

F♯m⁷   E   A   E
Blessed are the poor, the kingdom is theirs.

        C♯m⁷   F♯m⁷
Alive in the promise to be dead to the   world.

        E   A   E
Blessed are the meek in all of You Father,

A   E/B   E   A   E
The Word at Your right hand, spirit of truth.

CHORUS:

     A   E
Unwavering is Your voice,

    B   E
unwavering is Your hand,

     C♯m⁷   B/D♯   E
Unwavering is   the   heart

  C♯m⁷   B
that bled for the sins of man.

     A   E   B   C♯m⁷
Unwavering is Your will, unwavering is Your plan,

  A   E/B B
The fount of sal - vation

       (E   A   E) *last time C♯m⁷*
on which we will stand.

(B⁷ E A E C♯m⁷ A) *1st time only*

VERSE 2:

F♯m⁷   E   A   E
Blessed are the righteous on bended knee,

        C♯m⁷   F♯m⁷
Found in this freedom, committed to   You.

         E   A   E
Blessed are those who see the heights of glory,

A   E/B   B   E   A   E
Found in the valley,   and suffering for You.

(REPEAT CHORUS TWICE)

A   E/B
The fount of sal - vation

B   A   B   A   B
on which we will stand.

BRIDGE:

              A   B
Send us out to be Your hands and   feet,

              A   B
Send us out to be Your hands and feet,

              A   B
Send us out to be Your hands and   feet,

           A   B
Send us out to be Your hands and   feet.

              A   B
Send us out to be Your hands and   feet,

              A   B
Send us out to be Your hands and   feet,

              A   B
Send us out to be Your hands and   feet.

A B A B

Theme(s):
God's Attributes

Tempo:
dotted quarter 86 bpm
Mid Tempo

Played Key:
E

Vocal Range:

middle C

B - E

Similar Theme
Everything
Let God Arise

Similar Tempo
Everything Glorious
Made To Worship

Similar Key
Center
Strong Tower

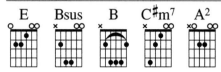
Scripture References

*John 3:16
For God so loved the world that he gave his one and only Son, that whoever beliees in him shall not perish but have eternal life.*

*John 14:6
Jesus answered, "I am the way and the truth and the life. No one comes to the Father except through me."*

Theme(s):
Peace & Hope

Tempo:
84 bpm
Mid Tempo

Played Key:
F

Vocal Range:

middle C

C - F

Similar Theme
Everlasting God
In Christ Alone

Similar Tempo
Sound Of Melodies
Unwavering

Similar Key
As We Seek Your Face
God Of Justice

While You Were Sleeping

MARK HALL

E   Bsus   B   C#m⁷   A²

Capo 1 (E)

VERSE 1:

```
E            Bsus        B         C#m⁷
   Oh, little town of Beth - lehem,          looks like
      A²       E    Bsus    B    C#m⁷   A²
an - other silent night.
E                    Bsus            B
   Above your deep      and dream - less sleep,
C#m⁷                A²
   A giant star    lights up the sky.
C#m⁷      A²    E                        Bsus       B
                   And while you're ly  -  ing in
         C#m⁷           A²             E
the dark,         There shines an ever last - ing light.
Bsus       B       C#m⁷            A²

E              Bsus        B
   For the King      has left   His throne,
C#m⁷            A²              E
   And is sleeping in a man - ger tonight, tonight.
Bsus       B       C#m⁷            A²

E              Bsus        B
   Oh, Bethlehem     what you  have missed,
C#m⁷                    A²          E
   While you were sleep - ing. For God became
      Bsus     B        C#m⁷               A²
a man,      And stepped into    your world today.
E              Bsus       B          C#m⁷
   Oh, Bethlehem      you will go down
        A²     E    a city    Bsus
in history,    as a city with no room
B        C#m⁷    A²                      E
for its King,              while you were sleep - ing,
Bsus       B       C#m⁷            A²

                E    Bsus    B    C#m⁷    A²
While you were sleep - ing.
```

VERSE 2:

```
E            Bsus        B         C#m⁷
   Oh, little town of Je - rusalem,        looks like
      A²       E    Bsus    B    C#m⁷   A²
an - other silent night.
         E                Bsus        B
The Father gave His on  -  ly son,
      C#m⁷                      A²
The Way, the Truth and the Life had come.
            E                Bsus        B
But there was no room for Him,
      C#m⁷                      A²
In the world He came to save.
E              Bsus        B
   Jerusalem     what you  have missed,
```

```
C#m⁷                    A²
   While you were sleep - ing.
E              Bsus    B       C#m⁷
The Savior of the world,     is dying on
        A²     E       Bsus       B
a cross today.      Jerusalem      you will go down
C#m⁷          A²     E          Bsus
   in history,    as a city with no room
B        C#m⁷    A²                      E
for its King,              while you were sleep - ing,
Bsus       B       C#m⁷            A²
                E    Bsus    B    C#m⁷    A²
While you were sleep - ing.
```

VERSE 3:

```
E            Bsus        B         C#m⁷
   United States of A - merica,        looks like
      A²       E    Bsus²   B    C#m⁷   A²
an - other silent night.
E                    Bsus            B
   As we're sound asleep      by phi - losophies,
C#m⁷                    A²          E
   That save the trees   and kill the chil - dren.
Bsus       B       C#m⁷            A²

E              Bsus        B          C#m⁷
   And while we're ly  -  ing there in the dark,
         A²             E       Bsus       B
There's a shout across the east - ern sky.
C#m⁷      A²    E          Bsus           B
                            For the Bride  -  groom has
      C#m⁷           A²                    E
returned,      and has carried His bride away
         Bsus     B        C#m⁷       A²
In the night,             in the night.
E              Bsus        B          C#m⁷
   America     what will  we miss      while we are
      A²     E       Bsus       B
sleep - ing? Will Jesus come again,      and leave
         C#m⁷           A²       E
us slum  -  bering where we lay?      America
Bsus       B       C#m⁷        A²       E
   will we go down    in history,    as a nation
         Bsus     B        C#m⁷       A²
with no room      for its King?
            E    Bsus    B    C#m⁷    A²
Will we be sleep - ing?
            E    Bsus    B    C#m⁷    A²
Will we be sleep - ing?
E              Bsus        B          C#m⁷
   United States of A - merica,        looks like
      A²       E    Bsus²   B    C#m⁷   A²
an - other silent night.
```

Wholly Yours
DAVID CROWDER

Key of (A)

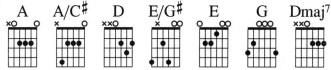

A   A/C#   D   E/G#   E   G   Dmaj⁷

Sheet Music available at WORSHIP TOGETHER.com

Scripture References

Romans 8:39
Neither height nor depth, nor anything else in all creation, will be able to separate us from the love of God that is in Christ Jesus our Lord.

VERSE 1:

A   A/C#   D
I am full of earth. You are heaven's worth.

A   A/C#   D
I am stained with dirt, prone to depravity.

A   A/C#   D
You are ev'rything that is bright and clean,

A   A/C#
The anto - nym of me. You are divinity.

PRE-CHORUS 1:

A/C#   D   A   E/G#
But a cer - tain sign of grace is this

A/C#   D   A   E/G#
From the bro - ken earth flowers come

E
Pushing through the dirt.

CHORUS 1:

      D   A   E
And You are ho - ly, ho - ly, ho - ly.

        D   A   E
All heaven cries, "Ho - ly, ho - ly God."

     D   A   E
Oh You are ho - ly, ho - ly, ho - ly.

       D   A   E
I want to be ho - ly like You are.

(A   A/C#   D) *1st time only*

VERSE 2:

A   A/C#   D   A
You are ev'rything that is bright and clean.

A   A/C#
And You're covering me with Your majesty.

PRE-CHORUS 2:

A/C#   D   A   E/G#
And the tru - est sign of grace was this:

A/C#   D
That from wound - ed hands

A   E/G#   E
Re - demption fell   down liberating man.

CONTINUED...

(REPEAT CHORUS 1)

BRIDGE:

G   D   A
But the harder I try the more clearly can I

                E/G#
Feel the depth of our fall

and the weight of it all.

D   A/C#
And so this might could be

            A
the most impossible thing:

             E/G#
Your grandness in me   making me clean.

D   A   E
Glo - ry, hal - lelujah.

   D   A   E
Glo - ry, glo - ry, hal - lelujah.

CHORUS 2:

       D   A   E
You are ho - ly, ho - ly, ho - ly,

        D   A   E
All heaven cries, "Ho - ly, ho - ly God."

       D   A   E
And You are ho - ly, ho - ly, ho - ly.

       D   A   E
I want to be ho - ly, ho - ly, God.

ENDING:

D   A   E
So here I am, all of me. Fi - nally ev'rything

     D   A   E
Whol - ly, whol - ly, whol - ly,

        D   A   E
I am whol - ly, whol - ly, whol - ly,

      D   A   E
I am whol - ly, whol - ly, whol - ly Yours.

A   A/C#   D

            A   A/C#   D
I am wholly Yours.

A   A/C#   Dmaj⁷
I am full of earth   and dirt and You.

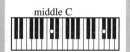

Theme(s):
Prayer & Renewal

Tempo:
150 bpm
Up Tempo

Played Key:
A

Vocal Range:

middle C

C# - F#

Similar Theme
I Want The Joy
Ready For You

Similar Tempo
Declare Victory
I Will Remember You

Similar Key
A Greater Song
I Will Remember You

Scripture References

*Matthew 16:24
Then Jesus said to his disciples, "If anyone would come after me, he must deny himself and take up his cross and follow me."*

*Matthew 6:10
Your kingdom come, your will be done on earth as it is in heaven.*

Theme(s):
Commitment & Dedication
Tempo:
75 bpm
Slow Mid-Tempo
Played Key:
G
Vocal Range:

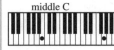

B - G

Similar Theme
For Your Glory
Hear Our Song

Similar Tempo
Be Lifted High
Unashamed

Similar Key
All We Need
Resurrection Day

Yes And Amen

MATT REDMAN, ROBERT MARVIN and JOSIAH BELL

KEY OF (G)

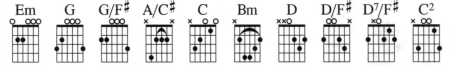

Em   G   G/F#   A/C#   C   Bm   D   D/F#   D⁷/F#   C²

VERSE 1:

Em
   Hear Your people saying yes,
                               G
Hear Your people saying yes   to You.
Em
   Yes to anything You ask,
                        G
Yes to anything we're called   to do.
Em
   Hear Your people say amen,
                        G
Hear Your people say amen   to You.
Em
   Let Your kingdom come on earth,
                      G
Let it be just like we prayed   to You.

CHORUS 1:

Yes and amen to everything that's in Your heart,
           G/F#
Yes and a - men to everything that You have planned.
     A/C#
We live to see Your will be done,
     C   G
And see Your perfect kingdom come on earth,
        Bm⁷
on the earth.

VERSE 2:

Em   D   Em
   All the promis - es are yes,
           D⁷/F#   G
All the promis - es are yes   in You.
Em   D   Em
   Every good and perfect gift,
                G
Every blessing that we have   was You.

(REPEAT CHORUS 1)

CONTINUED...

CHORUS 2:

                     G
Yes and a - men, we're taking up our cross for You.
                G/F#
Give us the strength to take these dreams

and follow through.
          A/C#
We live to see Your will be done,
          C   G
And see Your perfect kingdom come on earth,
           Bm*   *2nd time,* Bm⁷
On the earth.

VERSE 3:

Em   D   Em
   Hear Your people saying yes,
                D/F#   G   D/F# G Bm
Hear Your people saying yes   to You.
Em   D   Em
   Yes to any - thing You ask,
                D/F#   G   D/F# G Bm
Yes to any - thing we're called   to do.
Em   D   Em
   Hear Your people say amen,
                D/F#   G   D/F# G Bm
Hear Your people say amen   to You.
Em   D   Em
   Let Your kingdom come on earth,
                D/F#   G   D/F# G
Let it be just like we prayed   to You.

(REPEAT CHORUS 1 & 2)

G   D   G   C   G   C²   D/F#

Em   D/F#   G   D/F#   G   C/E   C²

ENDING:

(D/F#)*   Em   D/F#   G
Yes and a - men,
D/F#   G   C²
Yes and a - men.   *D/F# not played 1st time*

(REPEAT ENDING 3 TIMES)

D/F#   Em   D/F#   G

Yes You Have

LEELAND MOORING, JACK MOORING and MATT BRONLEEWE

Sheet Music available at
WORSHIP TOGETHER.com

KEY OF (E)

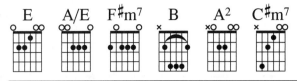

E   A/E   F#m⁷   B   A²   C#m⁷

Scripture References

*Psalms 66:4
All the earth bows down to You; they sing praise to You, they sing praise to Your name."*

(CONTINUED...)

VERSE 1:

E
   Ev'ry tree and ev'ry stone,
A/E
    Ev'ry rushing wind that moans,
   F#m⁷
They sing Your praise,
              E
My God they sing Your praise.

Ev'ry star and open sky,
A/E
    Tell of Your glory divine,
   F#m⁷
They shout Your praise,

They shout Your praise, yeah.

CHORUS:

B   E
   You've stolen my heart,   yes You have!
              A²
You've stolen my heart,   yes You have!
                       F#m⁷
You've wiped away the stains,
                    B   E
And broke away the chains,   yes, You have!

VERSE 2:

With Your love You set me free,
A/E
Three nails gave me liberty,
   F#m⁷
So I'll sing Your praise,
              E
My God I'll sing Your praise.

Oh, with Your love, You forgave my sin,
A²
   Forgot my past, and brought me back again.
   F#m⁷
So I'll sing Your praise,
   E
I'll sing Your praise, yeah.

(REPEAT CHORUS)

BRIDGE:

C#m⁷
       If I ascend into the sky,
E
   Or hide behind the night,
B   F#m⁷
   I cannot run, Your love   is chasing me.
A²
    If I fall into the sea,
C#m⁷
       Your hand will rescue me.
                        B
No one will take Your place, because
E
This is all for You,
       C#m⁷
Yes, this is all for You,

REFRAIN:

            A²   B
You're the king of the world,
            C#m⁷   B
You're the king of the world.

(REPEAT REFRAIN TWICE)

(REPEAT CHORUS TWICE)

ENDING:

E

Theme(s):
Love

Tempo:
92 bpm
Mid Tempo

Played Key:
E

Vocal Range:

middle C

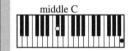

C# - B

Similar Theme
Carried To The Table
You Never Let Go

Similar Tempo
Give Me Jesus
Tears Of The Saints

Similar Key
Great God Of Wonders
Unwavering

You Are My God (Like A Whisper)

BRENTON BROWN

Scripture References

1 John 5:1
Everyone who believes that Jesus is the Christ is born of God, and everyone who loves the father loves his child as well.

Luke 18:17
I tell you the truth, anyone who will not receive the kingdom of God like a little child will never enter it."

KEY OF (E)

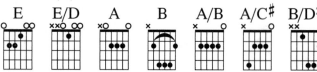

E   E/D   A   B   A/B   A/C#   B/D#

Theme(s):
Love

Tempo:
85 bpm
Mid Tempo

Played Key:
E

Vocal Range:

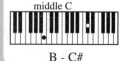

middle C

B - C#

VERSE 1:

E   E/D
  Like a whisper,   like a love song,

  A
I   can hear Your voice, I can hear Your voice.

E   E/D
  Like a father   to his newborn,

  A   E
I   can hear Your voice calling   me:

CHORUS 1:

            A   B   E
"You are My   child, you are My   child, and I love   you.

            A   B   E
You are My   child, you are My   child, and I love   you."

VERSE 2:

E   E/D
  Like a promise,   like a thank you,

  A
I   will sing this song, I will sing this song.

E   E/D
  For the way You   make my heart new,

  A   E
I   will sing this song to   You.

CHORUS 2:

            A   B   E
You are my   God, You are my   God, and I love   You.

            A   B   E
You are my   God, You are my   God, and I love   You.

BRIDGE:

          A   A/B
There is no   higher call, there's no great - er reward

          A/C#   A/B
Than to know   You, God, to be known   as Yours.

          A   A/B
There is no   better goal, nothing I'm   longing for

          A/C#   B/D#
Can compare   with the truth that forev - er more:

(REPEAT CHORUS 2)

You Never Let Go

MATT REDMAN and BETH REDMAN

KEY OF (A)

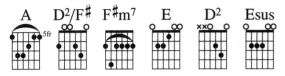

A   D²/F♯   F♯m⁷   E   D²   Esus

VERSE 1:

      A
Even though I walk through the valley

of the shadow of death,
   D²/F♯
Your perfect love is casting out fear.
      A
And even when I'm caught in the middle

of the storms of this life,
 D²/F♯
I won't turn back, I know You are near.

PRE-CHORUS:

      F♯m⁷ E A
And I will fear no e   -   vil,
      F♯m⁷ E A
For my God is with   me.
      F♯m⁷ E A
And if my God is with   me,
        E
Whom then shall I fear?
        D²
Whom then shall I fear?

CHORUS:

A
Oh no, You never let go,

Through the calm and through the storm.
F♯m⁷
Oh no, You never let go,

In every high and every low.
Esus
Oh no, You never let go,
D²   A   Esus   D²
Lord, You never let go of me.

CONTINUED...

VERSE 2:

        A
And I can see a light that is coming

for the heart that holds on,
   D²/F♯
A glorious light beyond all compare.
        A
And there will be an end to these troubles

but until that day comes,
   D²/F♯
We'll live to know You here on the earth.

(REPEAT PRE-CHORUS)

(REPEAT CHORUS TWICE)

VERSE 3:

        A
Yes, I can see a light that is coming

for the heart that holds on,
      F♯m⁷
And there will be an end to these troubles.
        Esus
But until that day comes   still I will praise You,
D²   A   Esus   D²
  still I will praise You.

(REPEAT CHORUS TWICE)

ENDING:

A

Theme(s):
Love

Tempo:
76 bpm
Slow Mid-Tempo

Played Key:
A

Vocal Range:

middle C

A - E

Similar Theme
See His Love
Yes You Have

Similar Tempo
As We Seek Your Face
Unashamed

Similar Key
Awesome Is The Lord
Most High
Wholly Yours

Scripture References

Psalms 104:31
May the glory of the Lord endure forever; may the Lord rejoice in his works.

Psalms 72:19
Praise be to his glorious name forever; may the whole earth be filled with his glory. Amen and Amen.

Your Glory Endures Forever

CHARLIE HALL

KEY OF (G)

C^2 Dsus   G^2/B   Am^7 D   G   G/F$^\sharp$ Em^7 A

VERSE:

C^2 Dsus   G^2/B   C^2
   And You ride on wings of wind, You are be - ginning and the end.

                  Dsus   G^2/B   Am^7
Mountains melting in Your flame, creation pulsing out Your name.

PRE-CHORUS:

             D
And You are forever,   and You are forever

CHORUS:

G   G/F$^\sharp$ C^2
   Your glory endures forever,   Your beauty out - shines the heavens.

Em^7 D   A   C^2
   And we will de - clare Your wonders,   Your splendor, Your   majesty.

VERSE:

          Dsus   G^2/B   C^2
Earth rotating in Your hand, galax - ies in Your com - mand.

                 Dsus   G^2/B   Am^7
You make and sustain the breath of man, Your deeds go on forever.

(REPEAT PRE-CHORUS)

(REPEAT CHORUS TWICE)

BRIDGE:

Am^7 Dsus   G^2/B   C^2
   You are forever,   You are forever,   You are forever,

Dsus   G^2/B   A   C^2
   You are forever,   You are forever,   You are forever.

(REPEAT CHORUS TWICE)

ENDING:

G   G/F$^\sharp$ C^2 Em^7 D   A   C^2

G   G/F$^\sharp$ C^2
Glory, and honor, and praise. Glory, and honor, and praise.

Em^7 D^2
Glory, and honor, and praise

C^2
   And You ride on wings of wind, You are beginning and the end.

Theme(s):
God's Attributes
Tempo:
dotted half note 54 bpm
Slow Mid-Tempo
Played Key:
G
Vocal Range:

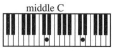

middle C

D - D

Similar Theme
Almighty God
Everything

Similar Tempo
Strong Tower
Uncreated One

Similar Key
All We Need
Hosanna
(Praise Is Rising)

Your Grace Is Enough

MATT MAHER and CHRIS TOMLIN

KEY OF (A)

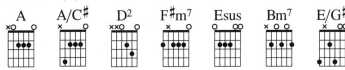

A   A/C♯   D²   F♯m⁷   Esus   Bm⁷   E/G♯

VERSE 1:

  A   A/C♯   D²
  Great is Your faithfulness, oh God

F♯m⁷   Esus   D²
  You wrestle with   the sinner's heart

  A   A/C♯   D²
  You lead us by   still waters into mercy

F♯m⁷   Esus   D²
  And nothing can   keep us apart

REFRAIN 1:

    Bm⁷   A/C♯   D²   Esus
So remember Your people, remember Your children

  F♯m⁷   A   D²
Remember Your promise, oh God

REFRAIN 2:

  A   Esus   F♯m⁷   D²
Your grace is enough,   Your grace is enough

  A   Esus   D²
Your grace is enough   for me

VERSE 2:

  A   A/C♯   D²
  Great is Your love   and justice, God

F♯m⁷   Esus   D²
  You use the weak   to lead the strong

  A   A/C♯   D²
  You lead us in   the song of Your   salvation

F♯m⁷   Esus   D²
  And all Your people sing along

(REPEAT REFRAIN 1 & 2)

(REPEAT REGRAIN 2)

REFRAIN 3:

    Bm⁷   A/C♯   D²   Esus
So remember Your people, remember Your children

  F♯m⁷   E/G♯   A   D²
Remember Your promise,   oh God

CONTINUED...

REFRAIN 4:

    A   Esus
  Your grace is enough

        F♯m⁷   D²
  Heaven reaching down to us

         A   Esus
  God I see Your grace is enough

    F♯m⁷   D²
  I'm covered in Your love

    A   Esus   F♯m⁷   D²
  Your grace is enough,   I'm covered in Your love

A   Esus   D²   A
Your grace is enough   for me for me

        Esus F♯m⁷   D²
(Spoken) For you,   for me for us. Hey!

A Esus   D²   A

9.0 Key Index

Song Title	Capo	Played Key	PAGE NUMBER Sheet Music	Enhanced Chord Charts
KEY OF A				
A Greater Song	2	G	2	251
Awesome Is The Lord Most High			29	257
I Will Remember You			121	276
Wholly Yours			210	295
You Never Let Go			230	299
Your Grace Is Enough			242	301
KEY OF A♭				
Declare Victory	1	G	63	264
Shine	1	G	162	285
Son Of God	1	G	168	286
KEY OF B				
All Over The World			18	253
Everything	4	G	80	266
Let God Arise	2	A	131	278
Tears Of The Saints	4	G	184	290
KEY OF B♭				
Almighty God	1	A	24	255
Closer	3	G	47	262
Everlasting God	3	G	70	265
How Can I Keep From Singing	1	A	116	275
KEY OF Bm				
See His Love			160	284
KEY OF C				
Beautiful Lord			38	259
Give Me Jesus			84	268
Jesus You Are Worthy			126	277
Made To Worship			136	279
Ready For You			144	281
Speak O Lord			178	288
KEY OF D				
Carried To The Table			42	260
Communion			58	263
Give You Glory			88	269
Hear Our Song			112	273
Outrageous Grace (There's A Lot of Pain)			142	280
Resurrection Hymn (See What A Morning)			152	283
Sound Of Melodies			172	287

9.0 Key Index

Song Title	Capo	Played Key	Sheet Music	Enhanced Chord Charts
			PAGE NUMBER	
KEY OF D♭				
Adoration	1	C	12	252
Everything Glorious	2	B	75	267
KEY OF E				
Center			52	261
Great God Of Wonders			93	271
Strong Tower			180	289
Unwavering			155	293
Yes You Have			217	297
You Are My God (Like A Whisper)			248	298
KEY OF E♭				
Uncreated One	1	D	198	292
KEY OF F				
As We Seek Your Face	3	D	28	256
God Of Justice	3	D	98	270
Unashamed	1	E	192	291
While You Were Sleeping	1	E	204	294
KEY OF F♯				
Hallelujah God Is Near			102	272
KEY OF G				
All We Need			7	254
Hosanna (Praise Is Rising)			107	274
Resurrection Day			148	282
Yes And Amen			224	296
Your Glory Endures Forever			236	300
KEY OF G♭				
Be Lifted High	2	E	34	258

9.0 Tempo Index

9.0 Tempo Index

9.0 Theme Index

9.0 Theme Index

	PAGE NUMBER	
THEME	SHEET MUSIC	ENHANCED CHORD CHARTS

9.0 Songs By Project

9.0 Songs By Project

WANNA PLAY?

These 5 songbooks will show you HOW TO.

From those who play by ear to the experienced music reader...
Now everyone can play today's top modern worship songs.

⭐ **Songbooks Include:**

Cut Capo Instruction & Charts - Immediately enhance your guitar sound by creating unique voicings with simple chord fingerings

Demo CD - Hear the verse, chorus and bridge of each song in a simple guitar/vocal recording

⭐ **And Of Course...**

Sheet Music - Standard notation for piano, vocal and guitar

Chord Charts - Lyric with chord names and diagrams

Overhead Masters and Key & Tempo Indexes